MY SOCIAL POWER!

**Social Confidence Guide:
For Boys & Girls
Tweens, Teens & Young Adults
Ultimate Social Success Toolkit!**

Conquer the Fear of Making Friends,
Teen Situations & Social Interactions

Part of the **MY POWER!** Series
Book 1

♥♥

SheriBelle Karper

Kingman Publications LLC

Copyright ©2025 by SheriBelle Karper

All rights reserved. Worldwide rights reserved.

No portion of this book may be reproduced in any form without written permission from the publisher or the author, except as permitted by U.S. copyright law. No part of this book may be reproduced, distributed, or transmitted in any form or by any means, including photocopying, recording, or other electronic or mechanical methods, without the prior written permission of the publisher or the author, except in the case of brief quotations embodied in critical reviews and certain other non-commercial uses permitted by copyright law.

This is a work of nonfiction. This publication is designed to provide accurate and authoritative information in regard to the subject matter covered. However, it is sold with the understanding that the author and the publisher are not engaged in rendering medical, legal, investment, accounting, doctoral, or other professional services. While the publisher and author have used their best efforts in preparing this book, they make no representations or warranties with respect to the accuracy or completeness of the contents of this book and specifically disclaim any implied warranties of merchantability or fitness for a particular purpose. The material provided is for informational, educational, and entertainment purposes only and should not be considered a substitute for professional advice or consultation from qualified authorities in the relevant fields. Readers should consult professionals or experts in specific areas for advice suited to their individual needs. No warranty may be created or extended by sales representatives or written sales materials. The advice and strategies contained herein may not be suitable for your situation. You should consult with a professional when appropriate. Neither the publisher nor the author assumes any responsibility or liability for any errors, omissions, or potential consequences from the application of the information provided within this book, nor shall they be liable for any loss of profit or any other commercial or personal damages, including but not limited to special, incidental, consequential, personal, or other damages.

Disclaimer: Names, characters, and incidents are either the product of the author's imagination or used fictitiously. Any resemblance to actual persons, either living or dead, events, or locales is purely coincidental.

ISBN: 978-1-967750-04-7 (paperback) • LCCN: 2025910281 (paperback)

ISBN: 978-1-967750-05-4 (ebook)

ISBN: 978-1-967750-16-0 (hardback)

ISBN: 978-1-967750-17-7 (audiobook)

Printed in the United States of America

1st Edition ©2025

Ultimate Empowerment Book to Excel In Teen Social Situations

MY SOCIAL POWER!

Social Confidence Guide

For Boys & Girls
Tweens, Teens and Young Adults

By SheriBelle Karper

FOR BOYS & GIRLS

Conquer the Fear of Making New Friends and Social Interaction

KP KINGMAN PUBLICATIONS

Contents

MY SOCIAL POWER!	1
Foreword By Dr. Renee Cotter, MD, OB/GYN, FACOG	7
Dedication	9
Epigraph	11
1. Welcome to MY SOCIAL POWER!	13
2. What is Social Confidence? (And Why Do You Need It?)	23
3. Cracking the Friendship Code	33
4. My Emotions Are Driving Me Crazy!	41
5. Social Media — Keeping It Cool and Positive	55
6. Tell Those Critics to Take a Hike! (Including the One Inside Your Head)	61
7. The Power of Setting Goals!	71
8. Everything In Life is Choices	79
9. Make a Difference with Your Review	87
10. The Mystery of Mean Girls (And Bullies)	89
11. "Dude, What's Up With These Mean Friendships?" (AKA, Mean Boys Are Real)	97
12. How Do You Try To Handle Mean Girls, Mean Guys, Bullies, and Cyberbullies?	109
13. The Peer Pressure Problem	121
14. Social Media Safety: We're Getting Real!	131
15. The Friendship Shift: Why is Everyone Acting So Weird?	141
16. Chill Out and Find Your Zen	145
17. Find Your People, Find Your Power!	155
18. Finding Your Squad of Superstars!	161
19. Your Social Spark: Bring on Your Own Personal Magic	167
20. Let's Talk About Something Super Cool: YOU!	173
21. Let's Shower the World with Kindness	179
22. Most Important Chapter in this Book, and I'm Not Kidding!	185
Acknowledgements	191
About the Author	193
Other Titles by SheriBelle Karper...	197

Glossary and Words to Know	199
Resources & References	203

Foreword By Dr. Renee Cotter, MD, OB/GYN, FACOG

As an obstetrician and gynecologist with over 30 years of experience in Southern California, I have dedicated my career to supporting women through the various stages of their lives. From the early years of puberty to the complexities of menopause, I have witnessed the profound physical and emotional changes that define womanhood. It is from this perspective that I wholeheartedly endorse SheriBelle Karper's invaluable guides *MY PERIOD POWER!, MY SOCIAL POWER!* and *MY BODY POWER!*

These books offer not just information, but a compassionate roadmap through the often daunting journey of puberty. SheriBelle masterfully navigates the physical transformations and the emotional landscapes that accompany this pivotal time, providing practical advice and heartfelt encouragement to help young adults embrace their evolving identities.

In *MY SOCIAL POWER!*, SheriBelle goes beyond the basics of physical care; she addresses the emotional and social challenges that can arise during this tumultuous period. Her insights into navigating social media and making safe choices are particularly relevant in today's digital age, where young teens face pressures that many of us from earlier generations can hardly imagine. By using language that resonates with young readers, SheriBelle ensures that her messages are not only accessible but also engaging.

Reflecting on my own experiences, I realize how fortunate I am to have grown up in a time without the influence of social media. After reading *MY BODY POWER!*, I realize again that conversations about menstruation or sexuality were often hushed, leaving many of us to navigate these changes in silence. *MY PERIOD POWER!* reminds me of the awkward moment of telling my mother I had started my period, only to receive a brief response about where to find pads. This lack of open dialogue fueled my passion for women's health and highlighted the necessity for clear, supportive resources.

MY PERIOD POWER!, MY SOCIAL POWER! and *MY BODY POWER!* are essential tools for young adults and should be seen as vital references for parents, educators, and healthcare professionals alike. They empower young readers to not only understand their bodies but to celebrate them. I envision a future where every young teen receives a copy of these books as a rite of passage, guiding them through the challenges of puberty with confidence and grace.

I encourage everyone who cares for or mentors young teens to embrace SheriBelle's work. Together, we can foster a generation of informed, empowered young adults who love themselves and their bodies.

Dr. Renee Cotter, MD, OB/GYN, FACOG

Dedication

To My Parents…
Thank you for the gift of curiosity.

♥

To the young girl in me who was shy…
Don't worry about it. It's all going to be fine.

♥

To my family…
I love you.

Epigraph

A girl should be two things: who and what she wants.
— Coco Chanel

♥

Be yourself; everyone else is already taken.
— Oscar Wilde

♥

I believe in being strong when everything seems to be going wrong. I believe that happy girls are the prettiest girls. I believe that tomorrow is another day, and I believe in miracles.
— Audrey Hepburn

♥

The trick is growing up without growing old.
— Casey Stengel

1. Welcome to MY SOCIAL POWER!

OK, real talk: Have you ever been walking down the hallway at school, feeling pretty cool… until you trip over *absolutely nothing*? And then you try to play it off like it was totally part of your plan? But your brain is like, "Let's re-live that moment 86 times in your head *just for fun!*" And, you're thinking, *Why am I like this?*

Or, have you ever been scrolling through social media, and it seems like everyone else is living in some epic movie moments—slow-motion hair flips, dream vacations, perfect group shots—while *you're* out there, just trying not to walk into a locker?

Yeah? SAME.

Let me tell you, you're not alone. Social life? It's basically like dodgeball—you're just trying not to get whacked in the face by the pressure. Growing up is also figuring out friendships and dealing with drama.

These are huge things. And that's exactly why I wrote **MY SOCIAL POWER!**

Why This Book Exists (Hint: It's for YOU!)

Let's be real: Life is messy, people are confusing, and middle school? Oh, it's just one endless episode of *Survivor*. Like, who even wrote these *rules?* Going through puberty, friendship drama, awkward moments, that awful "left out" feeling. And let's not forget the five million unspoken rules about how to act, post, look, breathe, and basically exist. It's enough to make anyone scream, "Can I just get a snack and a nap, please?!"

But guess what? You don't have to have it all figured out. Nope! What you do need is a sprinkle of confidence, a couple of tricks to handle the tough stuff, and a big scoop of self-love. Oh, and some laughs. (Laughing = instant life upgrade! Science says so!)

That's where **MY SOCIAL POWER!** comes in. Think of it as your all-in-one book, your best bud in a guide format; the kind of friend who hypes you up when you're feeling like a walking disaster. This book isn't about being perfect or pretending to be someone you're not. It's about embracing your quirks, loving who you are, and turning up the volume on your own inner awesomeness.

Not Your Average Book!

This book is written like you're chatting with your BFF or your best bro. We'll talk like real people with slang, jokes, and playful grammar. Because when you get something, you own it. And that's the goal here: Owning your social life by giving you real talk, real strategies, and real confidence. Win-Win-Win!

But hey, even though we're having fun, this is all super important information. It's written in a way that makes it easy to understand, interesting, and fun.

I Won't Talk Down to You

Here's my promise to you: I see you for the amazing person you're becoming. You're not a little kid. You're a tween or a teen who is just now stepping into your adult power, so I'm going to talk to you like that. There will not be any little kid talk because that's not who you are.

I will always speak to you with respect and keep it real. I'm all about positivity and helping you grow into the incredible adult you're becoming. You've got this, and I'm here to cheer you on every step of the way! Agreed? Yeah! Let's move on!

Your Place in Society is Changing... And That's a Good Thing!

You've probably noticed your body and mind a lot more lately. Maybe you're getting taller and your body is changing in all kinds of ways. Hello growth spurts, surprise smells are kicking in, and hair is showing up—yeah, *"down there"*— (Gaaaaah!) Maybe someone bought you deodorant, and suddenly, taking showers is a big deal. It's all normal. No need to feel awkward about all these changes. Everybody goes through it. I did. Your parents did. Even your grandparents did! Hard to picture, huh?

And here's the thing, your mind is changing, too. You're thinking about new things, asking bigger questions, and starting to wonder, *"Who do I want to be?"* You're starting to ask yourself these big adult-type questions, which means **you're starting to think about your social power!**

Congratulations! And welcome to the big show. Welcome to your NEW YOU!

Keeping It Cool and Confident

With all this body and mind action, you might also *feel* different on the inside, too. Maybe more excited, more grouchy, or more jittery about stuff than before. Totally normal and simply part of growing up.

So, What's Inside This Book?

We're going to define social confidence; what it actually means and how to grow yours.

- **The Magic of Making Friends** and how to develop your social confidence.
- **Tackling Comparisons:** We'll break down why social media can make us feel *less-than-great* and how to turn that around.
- **Self Expression and Diversity:** Because you're not here to fit in, you're here to shine.
- **Handling Stress and Emotions:** Growing up can feel like an emotional roller coaster. This book will help you handle that.
- **Dealing with Mean Girls and Guys, Bullies, Peer Pressure, and Cyberbullies:** Ugh, the worst, right? You'll learn how to deal with drama like a pro.
- **The Power of Choices and Kindness:** Your choices shape everything, and kindness is a secret superpower.
- **Building Your Support Crew:** finding the right friends and mentors that have your back.
- **Goal Setting and Decision-Making:** So you can go from "meh" to "HECK YEAH!" in anything you do.
- **Role Models and Inspiration:** Because the right influences can help you become your best self.

Welcome to MY SOCIAL POWER!

- **Dealing with Social Media** and how to handle it safely.

By the time you finish this book, you'll have all the tools to build your social confidence superpowers. That's so cool, isn't it?! Let's dive in!

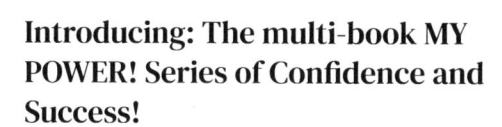

Introducing: The multi-book MY POWER! Series of Confidence and Success!

Meet Your Other MVPs: The Companion Books!

This book is part of the power packed MY POWER! confidence series! If you like **_MY SOCIAL POWER!_** (For All Tweens, Teens, and Young Adults), you'll have to check out:

MY BODY POWER! (For Girl Tweens, Teens, and Young Adults). It's a BODY CONFIDENCE GUIDE where you'll find answers to help you get to know and love your super special transforming body, and how to be proud of it in this fast-changing world.

You'll also want to get the other companion book to this one called **_MY PERIOD POWER!_** (For Girl Tweens, Teens, and Young Adults). It's a PERIOD CONFIDENCE GUIDE, where you'll learn everything you want and need to know about your period, dealing with guys, mood swings, stuff like that. We'll learn how to handle all these changes together and have a lot of fun along the way. You can get it at the same place you got this book. Super cool, eh?

Soon, there will be the ***MY PERIOD POWER! WORKBOOK*** (For Girl Tweens, Teens, and Young Adults) where you can journal, predict your period schedule, and monitor your moods, along with fun puzzles, recipes, and beautiful coloring pages. It will also be available wherever you got this book. Fun!

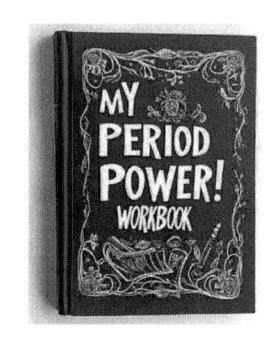

And, also the ***MY SOCIAL POWER! WORKBOOK*** (For Boy & Girl Tweens, Teens, and Young Adults) which will contain journaling, goal-setting, gratitude listing, prompts for writing, and other great things! This will also be available where you got this book.

This book contains the word "girl," "boy," "young man," and "young woman," and other gender-specific terms because I think that's who will probably read it. But hey, if those words don't fit with who you are, swap them out for words that fit you better. That way, you will still get all the awesome info in this book.

Think of This Book Like It's Your Best Friend

A friend who's got all the tips, tricks, and fun advice to help you totally own the social game. We're talking about everything from handling gossip to leading with confidence. We'll even do some quizzes and challenges to make it extra fun along the way. By the time you finish this book, you'll have all the tools to build your social confidence superpowers. Isn't that inspiring?! It will be fun!

By the time you read the last page in this book, you'll be a total pro about how YOU fit into this society's world. You'll know the ins and outs, the ups and downs, and all the science behind the magic. It's like

Welcome to MY SOCIAL POWER! 19

you'll become a social expert, and you'll be able to share what you've learned with your friends. This book will give you the courage to handle anything that comes your way. Pretty epic, right?

Now, Let Me Introduce Myself

I'm SheriBelle Karper, and I guess you could say helping people with their confidence is kind of what I do. If you check out the **About the Author** section at the back of the book (seriously, take a moment and read it later), you'll see I've done some pretty epic things in my life; things that you can totally do, too! Why? Because it all comes down to choices and figuring out what's important to you.

Anything is possible… or impossible… it all depends on how you look at life. I personally like the word *possible* much more than *impossible*. "Possible" gets you places. "Impossible" keeps you stuck.

Confidence isn't about knowing everything or being perfect. It's about showing up for yourself, trying new things (even when it feels scary), and embracing your fabulous, one-of-a-kind self. Mistakes? Whatever. They're just proof you're trying.

So, this book? It's all about helping you unlock the power you already have inside you. Yep, it's been there all along, like a treasure chest, waiting for you to crack it open. *You were actually born with everything you need.* Yes, everything is "possible."

Make sure you check out the amazing **Foreword written by Dr. Renee Cotter, OB/GYN!** I feel so honored that she wanted to be a part of this book, and she made her endorsement plainly clear in her phenomenal foreword. She's a very popular gynecologist and obstetrician for over 30 years in Los Angeles, California. So please, check it out!

It's Important To Ask Questions and Have Conversations

Got a question? Or are you super curious about something? That's great! Talk about it with your parents or trusted adult. They can even get their own copy of this book, and you both read along at the same time. You'll have some great and inspiring conversations. It will be low-key, AMAZING! Or maybe talk with a teacher or your doctor. Make sure it's someone that BOTH you AND your family trusts.

We'll get into all these topics and help you navigate them like a pro. You're awesome just the way you are, and this book will help you boost your social confidence even more. Imagine feeling totally in tune with all the changes going on around you and owning it. That's the goal!

Growing up, dealing with social issues, and mastering all those changes is like unlocking a superpower. Sure, it might feel like a lot at first, but once you own it, you'll feel unstoppable. Think about it: Knowing all this about your social power puts you in control.

I Know It's a lot of Information But There's an Old Saying

"Rome wasn't built in a day."

Don't worry, we're not about to go out and build a city! Hahaha, no! What we are going to do is build your internal social map. But it's a huge project that is impossible to handle all at once.

1. **We're going to break it down** and take each word, each idea, each building block, one brick at a time.

2. **We'll learn and apply** each concept, assembling them piece by piece.
3. **Then, we'll use all of it to build yourself** into your most amazing YOU!!

Whew! So how about we get this party started?! Grab a cozy spot, keep an open mind, and get ready to discover how awesome you truly are. Let's go find that amazing, unstoppable YOU that you were born to be! Are you ready? **Your social power is waiting!**

ACTION TAKEAWAYS:

- This is not your average book. It's written like how people talk to each other.
- Our differences are our superpower! Those little quirks and things that make you different? That's what makes you fantastic! Don't hide them, rock them!
- You're growing into something amazing! Change is good, but sometimes change is not always easy.
- Get ***MY BODY POWER!*** (For Girl Tweens, Teens, and Young Adults), ***MY PERIOD POWER!*** (For Girl Tweens, Teens, and Young Adults), the ***MY SOCIAL POWER! WORKBOOK*** (For Boy & Girl Tweens, Teens, and Young Adults), and the ***MY PERIOD POWER! WORKBOOK*** (For Girl Tweens, Teens, and Young Adults) to help you through these big changes in your life.
- Ask questions and get answers. Be a good listener and make sure you hear the answers correctly and then work that great advice into your life.

2. What is Social Confidence? (And Why Do You Need It?)

What Social Confidence Is:

Before we jump into becoming the social wizard you're destined to be, let's break down what social confidence actually is.

- **Feeling good about who you are,** whether you're with one person or a whole crowd.
- **Finding your inner glow** that helps you walk into a room and say "Hi" without freaking out.
- **Being able to talk to people** without worrying about what they will think of you.
- **Knowing how to handle awkward moments** (because, let's be honest, they happen to everyone).
- **Laughing at yourself** when you mess up (because everyone does).
- **Saying "NO"** when something doesn't feel right.
- **Being kind to others,** but not being a doormat.
- **Having tools** to use when dealing with mean people.

- **Quieting your inner critic** so you can rock this world!

It's not about being perfect or saying all the right things, it's about believing that you're pretty amazing, just as you already are. It's like having an invisible force field of self-belief that makes you feel comfortable in your own skin, no matter who you are with.

What Social Confidence is *NOT*

It's not about being the loudest person in the room. Nope. Or, the kid who always has the funniest jokes. Yeah, not that either. It's not about being bossy or thinking that you're better than everyone else. No, social confidence is way cooler than that…

Social confidence means trusting yourself to handle people and situations, even when you're feeling a little nervous. It's about treating yourself and other people with respect, and relaxing into your social moments with ease and grace. And let me tell you, this takes practice.

IMPORTANT INSIGHT:

You can be shy and still have social confidence. Likewise, you can be bold and really not have much self-confidence at all. Confusing, right? Sometimes bold people are overcompensating to make up for their lack of social confidence.

Why Do You Need Social Confidence?

Here's the deal: Life is full of situations where social confidence comes in really handy:

- **Talking to new people** (without your brain going blank).

What is Social Confidence? (And Why Do You Need It?)

- **Standing up for yourself** (even when your voice shakes a little).
- **Feeling okay if someone doesn't like you** (Because newsflash: Not everyone will like you, and that's okay!)
- **Surviving group projects**, social dances, oral presentations, and family reunions like a total pro.
- **Communicating with others** about what you believe in.
- **Trying new things** without worrying about looking silly or feeling uncomfortable.

When you're socially confident, you don't have to fake it. All you need to do is show up as the awesome person you already are. And the best part? Social confidence is a skill that you can learn and build step-by-step. And let's face it, social confidence makes life easier and a lot more fun.

The Totally Not-Scary, Super-Amazing, 100% Real Guide to Social Confidence

Okay, so picture this: You're at a party. There's music, snacks (hopefully pizza, or what is even the point?!), and a bunch of kids talking and laughing. Everyone looks like they know exactly what they're doing. Meanwhile, you're standing there, clutching a cup of soda like it's a lifeline, wondering if you should just make a dramatic exit and pray nobody notices.

Here's the secret: Social confidence is the magical thing that makes you feel like you *belong* at that party instead of wanting to disappear into the snack table. And no, you don't have to be the boldest, funniest, most popular person in the room to have it. All you need is a few tricks up your sleeve. Lucky for you, I have many *sleeves* and *many* tricks.

Step 1: The "I Totally Belong Here" Stance

Even if your brain is screaming, "AAAAAAH! WHAT DO I DO?!" Just pretend like you've been there before. Stand up straight, keep your arms relaxed (no T-Rex hands!), and remember that *nobody* is thinking about *you* as much as *you* are thinking about *you*. Seriously, people are too busy worrying about their own stuff, like if there's something stuck in their teeth.

Step 2: The Magic of "Hey!"

Do you want to start a conversation but don't know how? Let me introduce you to a magical, all-powerful, conversation-starting word: **"Hey."**

- "Hey! What's up?"
- "Hey! Your sneakers are cool."
- "Hey! Have you tried the pizza yet? Because I'm about to have some, and I need to know if I'm about to have a life-changing experience."

Boom! Conversation = Started.

Step 3: The Art of Not Being Weird About It

Talking to new people can feel like trying to diffuse a bomb while blindfolded. But actually, it's not that deep. Try to be chill. (Easier said than done, I know!) Ask people about themselves, laugh when something's funny, and don't overthink every single little thing you say.

For example:

- **Good:** "Hey! Cool hoodie. Where'd you get it?"
- **Not So Good:** "Hi, hello, greetings fellow human. I have arrived at this social event."

Step 4: The Confidence Cheat Codes

Do you want to know a secret? Confidence isn't about knowing everything or never feeling nervous. It's about acting like you're chill even when your brain is doing backflips. The trick? **Fake it 'til you make it.**

Try this: Before you walk into a room, tell yourself, **"I am cool. I've got this. I am, in fact, THE moment."** Even if you don't believe it at first, your brain will eventually go, "Oh! Okay, I guess we've got this!"

Step 5: The "It's Okay to Be Awkward" Clause

Everybody, and I mean everybody, has done something awkward in public. Maybe you wave at someone who wasn't waving at you. Maybe you say "You too!" when the waiter tells you to enjoy your meal. Maybe you trip over your own feet while standing still. IT HAPPENS. Just laugh it off and move on.

Step 6: Be You (Unless You're a Lizard in Disguise… Then Maybe Don't.)

What's the absolute best way to have social confidence? **Be yourself.** You don't have to change your personality to fit in. If you love books, talk about books. If you love skateboarding, talk about that. If you think sharks are the best animals ever and want to discuss why they are misunderstood ocean puppies, then go FIND YOUR PEOPLE!

How Does Social Confidence Work in Today's World?

Okay, here's the deal: Social confidence in today's world is a little different from what it was for your parents (or your teachers). Why? Because of social media. Yep, TikTok, Instagram, and whatever new app comes out next week all play a big role in how we see ourselves and how we connect with others.

It's like having two worlds to deal with:

1. **The Real World** (You know: School, sports, friends, gaming, sleepovers).
2. **The Online World** (Snapchat streaks, posting selfies, and texting your best friend memes).

Social confidence is about feeling good in *both* worlds. It's about knowing:

- Not everything you see online is real (filters, and perfect-looking lives).
- You don't have to compare yourself to everyone else.
- Your worth isn't based on how many likes or *followers* you have.

IMPORTANT INSIGHT:

Your real world is way more important than your online world. ALWAYS.

Quiz: How Socially Confident Are You Right Now?

Let's figure out where you're at right now on your social confidence game! Circle the answer that sounds most like you, and let's see what your results say.

What is Social Confidence? (And Why Do You Need It?)

1. You're at a party, and you only know one person. What do you do?

   A. Stick to them like glue and pray nobody else talks to you.
   B. Say "hi" to a couple of people, but mostly hang out in the corner.
   C. Introduce yourself to a few new people, and ask them about their favorite hobbies.
   D. Start a dance-off in the middle of the room, because, why not?

2. Someone asks you to join a group project. How do you feel?

   A. Terrified. What if I mess up or say something dumb?
   B. Nervous, but willing to give it a shot.
   C. Eager to help and share ideas (but also a little nervous).
   D. Thrilled! *This is my time to shine.*

3. You accidentally trip in the hallway and people notice. What do you do?

   A. Pretend it never happened and hope nobody remembers.
   B. Smile awkwardly and keep walking.
   C. Laugh and say, "Well, *that* was graceful!"
   D. Bow and say, "Thank you! Thank you! I'll be here all week!"

4. Someone you don't know very well says "hi" to you. What do you do?

   A. Panic and mumble "hi" back without making eye contact.
   B. Say "hi" and hope they keep walking.
   C. Smile, say "hi," and ask them how their day is going.
   D. Start a whole conversation and make them laugh within 30 seconds.

Results:

Mostly A's: The Social Caterpillar

You're only starting out on your social confidence journey, and that's OK! You might feel nervous in new situations, but with a little practice, you'll be branching out like a social rockstar in no time.

Mostly B's: The Quiet Observer

You're just beginning to warm up to the social game. You're polite and friendly, but still finding your comfort zone. Keep stepping out of your shell, and your confidence will soar.

Mostly C's: The Friendly Firecracker

You've got a solid handle on social confidence! You're approachable, fun, and great at connecting with people. You might have a couple of things to learn about social confidence, but you're open to suggestions.

Mostly D's: The Social Superstar in Training

Well, look at you! You're brimming with confidence and *seem* ready to take on a lot of social situations. Remember to help others feel included too, because your energy is contagious.

Since we now know where you are in the social game, let's get on this radical journey of building your social confidence. Even if you were the social superstar in the quiz above, there's still a lot to learn about how to maneuver in this social atmosphere we call life.

Here's the big secret: Social confidence starts *inside*. It's not about wearing the trendiest clothes or being the most popular kid in school. It's about deciding that you're awesome, flaws and all. Because everyone has flaws. Everyone. Even the people who seem like they have it all together have things they wish were different.

So next time you're in a tricky situation, remember this: You don't have to be perfect. You just have to be *you*. And that? That's more than enough.

Do I Really Need to Know All This Stuff?

It's a really good idea to learn self-confidence when you're younger, because you're really going to need it when you get older. So, you might as well start practicing it now! Having self-confidence when you're an adult can make or break your career. And, since I'm sure you're going to want to *"kill it"* in everything you do, let's dive into this social confidence thing headfirst so we can give your future the best possible outcome we can!

Ready to Rock This? ROCK ON!

ACTION TAKEAWAYS:

- Social confidence is feeling good about who you are.
- Social confidence is NOT about being the loudest or funniest person in the room.
- It's okay to be awkward.
- Fake it until you make it.
- Try out the magical word, "Hey!"
- You can be shy and still be socially confident!
- When we talk about social confidence, we're talking about the real world AND the online world.
- Social confidence starts on the inside.
- We need to practice social confidence now so that we will have it pretty much perfected by the time we're adults.
- Social confidence helps with your future.

3. Cracking the Friendship Code

Let's talk about something that's basically the cheat code for life: **Friendship.** The people you click with, laugh with, cry with (or just share your chips with at lunch) are like the Wi-Fi of your soul. When you've got a strong connection, everything works and feels better. But friendships can also get messy—like that awkward moment when you have that "I didn't mean to say that" messy. Don't worry, here is the ultimate guide to building and keeping the kind of friendships that make your life sparkle.

The Friendship Code

Getting along and making friends can feel a little like learning a dance. It's all about timing, rhythm, and not stepping on someone else's toes. Here's your secret code to unlocking awesome friendships:

- **Be yourself** (and not some watered-down version). Real friends love you for YOU, even if you snort-laugh or cry over an animal rescue video. Pretending to be someone else to fit in might work for a little while, but it will never feel as good as finding people who care about the real you, quirks and all.
- **Show up:** Say "hi," start conversations, and invite people to do stuff. Sometimes making friends is as simple as saying, "Hey, want to sit together?" or "Let's hang out!" Being friendly and approachable is like sending out good vibes that people want to catch.
- **Be curious:** Ask questions about other people's lives. People love it when you genuinely want to know their favorite pizza topping or their secret talent. It shows you care about who they are, not only what they can do for you.
- **Appreciate them:** Say thank you when they're awesome (which is probably a lot). Gratitude goes a long way in making your friends feel valued and uplifted.

Building Healthy Relationships

Okay, so you've met someone who could be a friend, now what? Relationships, whether they're your crew, study buddies, or teammates, need some tender loving care to grow strong. Think of them like a plant. (Yes, you're a friendship gardener now.)

- **Water it with kindness:** Say nice things, give sincere compliments, and celebrate their wins. When your friend nails a presentation or scores a goal, let them know how awesome they are. A little kindness can go a long way in keeping your connection healthy.

- **Give it sunshine:** Spend quality time together. This doesn't have to be anything fancy. A walk, a quick video chat, or even just sitting together at lunch counts. The point is to let them know they're important to you.
- **Pull the weeds:** Keep negativity and drama out. If something is bothering you, talk about it calmly instead of letting it fester. And if they are the ones stirring the pot, gently set some boundaries.

What Makes a Good Friend?

Good friends are like your favorite snacks—reliable, satisfying, and always a mood booster. Here are the green flags (the good things) to look for:

- **They listen:** Like, really listen. Not just nodding while scrolling through TikTok. A good friend hears what you're saying and cares about how you're feeling.
- **They're trustworthy:** If you tell them something private, it stays private. No exceptions. Knowing you can trust someone is the foundation of any great friendship.
- **They are supportive:** Whether you're chasing a dream, surviving math class, or simply trying to get through the day, they're in your corner cheering you on. A good friend wants to see you win.

Red Flags vs. Green Flags

Here's a quick guide to spotting healthy friendships versus ones that might not be so great:

- **Green Flags:** Kindness, honesty, mutual respect, laughing till your stomach hurts. These are all signs of a friendship that is healthy and worth your time and energy.
- **Red Flags:** Gossiping about you, lying, making you feel bad about yourself, or being a drama magnet. If someone's behavior constantly leaves you feeling drained or upset, it's okay to figure out if the friendship is right for you.

If someone's waving more red flags than a soccer referee, it might be time to rethink the friendship and move on. Your energy and time are precious. Don't waste them on people who don't deserve it.

Handling Jealousy, Misunderstandings and Tough Moments

Even the best friendships hit some bumps. Jealousy? Misunderstandings? Awkward moments? Ugh, we've all been there. Here's how to deal with it:

- **Jealousy:** If you're feeling left out or jealous, talk about it. A simple, *"Hey, I've been feeling kind of weird lately"* can work wonders. Be honest about your feelings without accusing or blaming.
- **Misunderstandings:** Don't let small stuff turn into big drama. Clarify what happened and give each other grace. Sometimes it's just a case of getting the wrong information, and a quick conversation can clear things up.
- **Tough moments:** If your friend's going through something hard, just listen. You don't need to have all the answers. Sometimes being there for them is enough. A simple "I'm here for you" can mean the world to them.

How to Apologize and Make Things Right

Did you mess up? It happens. The key is owning up to it and making it right. Here's the apology formula:

- **Say it straight:** "I'm sorry for _____." Be specific. Don't dodge the issue or make excuses. Own up to what you did.
- **Acknowledge the hurt:** "I understand how that might've made you feel." Showing empathy is a big part of a genuine apology.
- **Make it right:** "How can I fix this?" This shows you're committed to making things better and repairing the friendship.

Boom! Apology accepted (hopefully).

Drama Starters, Cliques, and Gossip

Ugh, drama demons are like those over-the-top villains in movies. They thrive on creating chaos and making everything about them. Then there are cliques—those little "exclusive clubs" that act like the school hallway is their own VIP section. And don't get me started on gossip. It's like a bad game of *Telephone* where everybody loses.

Here's the deal: Those drama dogs, cliques, and gossip hounds only have power if you give it to them. The best way to deal? **Don't feed the drama monsters!**

- **Be drama-free:** Keep your cool and don't engage. If someone says, "Did you hear what Jordan did?!" respond with, "Nah,

I'm not into that stuff."—BOOM!—you just walked away with your dignity intact.
- **Be kind to everyone** (even the drama queens and kings). Sometimes, being nice throws them off their game. (Seriously, they won't know what to do with it.)
- **Find your people:** Hang out with friends who lift you up and don't make you prove yourself just to hang out with them at lunch. True friends don't do drama. They do snacks, laughs, and good vibes.

Why Drama Exists and How to Avoid It

Here's the secret: Drama exists because people need attention, and stirring up trouble is an easy way to get it. It's like the glitter of the social world; it looks flashy, but it sticks to everything and is impossible to clean up.

How to avoid it?

- **Stay neutral:** If someone tries to drag you into their drama, just say, "I'm not picking sides. I like everyone." Neutrality = Peace.
- **Don't be the spark:** Don't spread rumors, stir the pot, or fan the flames. Instead, focus on your own glow-up.
- **Avoid the traps:** Drama lives in group texts, vague social media posts, and whispers in the hallway. Don't let them pull you in.

What to Do if You're Pulled Into Gossip

Sometimes, you're just minding your own business when gossip tries to suck you in like a vacuum. Don't panic—you've got this.

Cracking the Friendship Code

- **Pause before you speak:** Before you say anything, think: "Would I want someone saying this about me?" If the answer is no, then don't say anything.
- **Shut it down:** You don't have to be rude. A simple, "I'm not comfortable talking about them" helps a lot.
- **Change the subject:** "Did you see the new Marvel movie?!" or "What's everyone bringing to the bake sale?" will shift the convo faster than you can say "cookies."

When It's Time to Let Go

Not all friendships are forever, and that's OK. If someone's always bringing you down or crossing boundaries, it might be time to let them go. Here's how:

- **Be honest:** Explain how you feel. You don't have to be mean, just be real. Something like, *"I feel like our friendship isn't healthy for me right now"* can open the conversation.
- **Take space:** If talking doesn't work, it's okay to step back. Focus on the friendships that bring you joy.
- **Focus on the positive:** Let go and make space for better friendships to grow. It's not about holding grudges, it's about protecting *your peace*.

You've Got This!

Friendship isn't always easy, but it's SO worth it. With a little effort, a lot of kindness, and some good vibes, you can build relationships that lift you up and make life awesome. So go out there, crack the code, and build your social power one amazing friendship at a time!

ACTION TAKEAWAYS:

- Having friends is the magic of life. It's important to know how to make friends.
- When making friends, the most important thing you can do is to relax and be yourself.
- Good friends listen, are trustworthy, and supportive.
- Look for hints whether this person is right for you. Do they do they lift you up, or do they gossip, lie, or create a lot of drama?
- It's important to know how to apologize when you hurt someone.
- Life is easier if you have drama-free relationships.
- Sometimes, friendships just don't work out. It's important to know that it's okay to walk away.
- If you're having problems with your friendships, talk about it with your parents, siblings, or even a teacher. If it's bothering you, talk it out.

4. My Emotions Are Driving Me Crazy!

Okay, let's be real. Emotions feel like A LOT.

Yeah, I hear you! You're up, you're down, you're in, you're out, you're in this giant whirlwind of emotions, and it can WEAR YOU OUT.

The truth? This whirlwind? It's normal.

Right now, during all these changes in your life, it isn't just about knowing what to say or how to act, it's also about how you feel inside.

You could have the funniest jokes, the best hair day ever, and the kind of charisma that makes people want to follow you in the hallways like you're leading a parade. But, if you're feeling awkward, anxious, or down on yourself? Yeah, during those times, your social power isn't going to shine as brightly.

Growing up isn't just about getting taller or dealing with breakouts; your emotions are going through a full-on software update, too. One minute you're so relaxed, and the next, you're spiraling because someone gave you a *look*. (*What does it mean? Is there something on my face? Are my socks weird? Am I weird???*)

Here's the thing: Everyone feels this way sometimes. Your brain is basically remodeling itself, like a house under construction, except instead of new countertops, you're getting new ways to think, feel, and act. But, don't worry, I've got you!

Feeling Good on the Inside = Social Confidence Superpower!

Ever have one of those days where you feel unstoppable? You're making people laugh, walking with purpose, and just shining like the universe?

And then the next day, you trip over your own feet, forget how to be human, and say something so *cringe* that you replay it in your head for eternity?

Yeah, welcome to being alive.

Here's the deal:

- **Your emotions control your confidence.** When you feel good, you carry yourself confidently. You talk more, laugh more, and connect with people more.
- **Your confidence affects your social game.** When you're comfortable in your skin, you're not overthinking every little thing, you're just being YOU.
- **Your social confidence also affects your emotions.** When you have positive connections with other people, your brain says, "Nice! Let's do that again!" Moments like that are when your confidence grows.

My Emotions Are Driving Me Crazy! 43

But when you're having those crummy *"I'm so down on myself"* moments, your social confidence is going to have a rough day.

See the pattern? Emotions, confidence, and social life are like best friends who rely on each other to cheer each other on.

Sooooo... Let's Talk About Controlling Those Emotions

Here's a **TRUTH BOMB**...

Are you ready for it?

YOUR EMOTIONS ARE A CHOICE.

And, you can *CHOOSE* how you want to feel.

Did I just blow your mind? Aren't those statements kind of **AMAZING?**

I know, I know, it doesn't feel like that sometimes, but it's 100% true. If someone says something mean, it feels like you have no control over your reactions, and that reacting badly to it is the only choice. But here's the secret:

While you can't always control what happens around you, you *can* control how you react.

Do you want to let your emotions rule you? Probably not, because emotions can be exhausting. Sooo... since your emotions are a choice you can make, you can choose a different emotion. (WHAAAT?) Seems too simple, right? Well, it is, and it isn't. It takes practice to turn those bad feelings off like a light switch, and it's definitely not easy. But you can't do it until you try, so why not start today? If you're sad, despite your sadness, you can choose to be happy... or grateful.... or helpful… or strong… or _____… Fill in the blank and just be it.

If you're feeling frustrated, you can *choose* to feel determined.

If you're feeling left out, you can *choose* to remind yourself of your worth.

If you're feeling awkward, you can *choose* to laugh it off.

It takes practice to flip those emotions off like a light switch, but once you start, it gets easier every time.

PERSONAL SIDE STORY:

So, there was this one time at school when I totally bombed a quiz. Like, big time. I felt that familiar wave of frustration and embarrassment creeping in, and I was ready to let it ruin my whole day. But then, something clicked.

Instead of letting those bad feelings take over, I *decided* to take a deep breath and try something different. I told myself, "Okay, I messed up. I can either mope about it or use it as a chance to learn." It wasn't easy, but I **chose** to shake off the negativity and focus on what I could do better next time.

It was kind of like flipping a switch. I realized I didn't have to be stuck feeling crummy; I had the power to decide how I wanted to feel. I could choose to be upset, or I could choose to feel okay and see it as a learning experience. And once I made that choice, everything felt lighter.

So yeah, emotions can be tricky, but we get to decide how we handle them. Next time something goes wrong, just try to *flip that switch*. You might be surprised how much better you'll feel!

Emotions and Your Self-Esteem

Let's be real: Emotions can be draining. One minute you're on top of the world and the next you're drowning in all the feels because your best friend didn't say "hi" to you at lunch. The thing is, emotions aren't bad. They're like little clues that tell us what's going on inside. And when you learn how to handle them, you'll start glowing from the inside out. So grab your emotional highlighter and let's light up that inner glow because it's time to work on your shine.

Let's Work on Your Inner Glow

Your inner glow is like a superpower—it's what makes you feel confident, happy, and ready to take on the world. But it doesn't simply show up like magic. You've got to create it!

Start By Speaking Kindly to Yourself

You wouldn't tell your best friend they're terrible at life, would you? Of course not! So don't do it to yourself. Try saying, "I've got this," or "I'm proud of how hard I'm trying." Positive Vibes = Major Glow.

Time to Kick Those Bad Thoughts Out!

Here's a bit of insight: **Your brain believes what you tell it the most.** All those repeating thoughts of doom and gloom swirling in your head? Yeah, after hearing that same negativity on repeat, your brain starts to believe it. If that's all it hears, what else is it supposed to think?

So, maybe start telling it something good instead!

How to Make Your Brain Your Best Cheerleader!

- **Catch those negative thoughts.** Notice when your brain is being a total *hater* and tell it to *relax*.
- **Flip the script.** Instead of "I'm bad at this," try "I'm getting better every time I try."
- **Practice makes perfect.** The more you cheer yourself on, the more natural it feels.

Liking Yourself

You spend more time with yourself than anyone else in the world. So, it's a good time to actually start liking yourself! But how?

- **Focus on your strengths:** You've got amazing qualities, even if you don't always see them. Maybe you're a great listener or an epic artist. Only you know what those awesome qualities are until you let them out and show them to the world. Celebrate what makes you awesome.
- **Accept your quirks:** Nobody is perfect, and honestly, perfect is boring. Whether you have a silly laugh, or can't eat cereal without spilling your milk, your quirks are what make you unique. Own them!
- **Be your own cheerleader with positive self-talk:** Treat yourself the way you treat a good friend. When you're struggling, remind yourself that you're doing your best, and that's pretty great.

The Secret to Social Power? Positive Self-Talk.

It's so cool that you can train that voice inside your head to be super nice instead of having negative thoughts! Like, imagine it cheering you on and telling you how awesome you are. It's all about turning your thoughts upside down and making your inner voice your number-one fan. Let's get those good vibes going with positive self-talk!

What is Self-Talk?

Your brain is always talking to you. (I know, creepy, right?) The question is… What's it saying?

Self-talk is basically the stuff you tell yourself inside your head all day long. It has the ability to shape your self-esteem, with both positive and negative results.

- **Positive Self-Talk:** This is when your voice is all about good stuff! Like, "I can totally do this!" and "I look great today!" and "I'm a good friend!"
- **Negative Self-Talk:** This is when your thoughts are being a total downer. Things like: "I'm not good at this," or "I can't wear that," or "No one likes me." Those statements can make you feel horrible, big time. So, let's try some positive self-talk instead.

Exercises to Build Self-Esteem and Master Positive Self-Talk

- **Notice the Negatives:** Start noticing when you say mean things to yourself. Try to catch those negative thoughts and imagine stopping them like a red traffic light. You can literally say "STOP!" Or "NO!" inside your head. If you can say no in

other parts of your life, you can also say no to negative thoughts.
- **How You Talk to Yourself:** Turn those negatives into positives. Instead of saying, "I'm not good at this," try saying, "I'm getting better every single time I try this."
- **Practice Makes Perfect:** The more you practice positive self-talk, the more natural it will feel. It's like being your own cheerleader.
- **Daily Affirmations:** Every morning, say something nice about yourself. You can even go into your bathroom and look at yourself in the mirror and say these things. When you repeat them over and over, it helps them sink in. Like, "I'm feeling great today!" or "I totally rocked that guitar solo!" Put these great affirmations on paper and tape them to your mirror or put sticky notes on your laptop or notebook. You can even decorate them! Because when you see them all the time, someday soon, those great thoughts will sink into that awesome head of yours!
- **Talk to Yourself Like You Would a Best Friend:** Think about how you talk to your friends when they feel down. You wouldn't say mean things, right? Talk to yourself the same way that you would talk to your best friends.

Positive Affirmations You Can Repeat Daily

- "I'm proud of myself for trying my best."
- "I am worthy of kindness and respect."
- "I'm allowed to make mistakes. That's how I learn."
- "I'm brave, strong, and capable."
- "Today is a new day, and I've got this!"
- "I'm enough, just as I am."

My Emotions Are Driving Me Crazy!

- "I'm a good friend, and I attract good friends."
- "I'm creative, smart, and full of great ideas."
- "I believe in myself and my dreams."
- "I'm unique and that's my superpower."

Try these out or create some of your own. The list is endless!

REMEMBER:

When you say something, whether it's to a friend or just inside your mind, guess who is the first person to hear it?—YOU. So, make sure your words are kind to yourself and others. It will make your day feel great and you'll feel so much happier.

Why Positive Self-Talk Rocks!

- **Positive Self-Talk Boosts Your Confidence Level:** It helps you believe in yourself. Give yourself a good cheerleading session and you'll feel ready to take on the world!
- **Positive Self-Talk Reduces Stress:** When you're nicer to yourself, you feel less stressed. It's like giving your mind a big, cozy hug.
- **Positive Self-Talk Helps You Do Better:** Believing in yourself helps you do better in school, sports, and life. It's like your own secret superpower!

Here's a Secret…

Adults do positive self-talk, too! Sometimes, before going into a big meeting where there's a lot at stake, people walk into the bathroom, look in that mirror, and talk themselves up like the superstars they are. You can do this, too. The point is, this great pattern of cheering yourself on is something that you can do now, like right this minute. By mastering positive self-talk now, you'll be unstoppable when you're an adult!

The Seven-Day Positivity Challenge!

For the next week, end each day by writing nice things down in a journal or on paper (just not on your phone). Write three positive things you said to yourself that day. Each day, look back on the day before. See how much better you will feel after only one week!

You'll say, "Wow! Who is this Rockstar? I want to know that person!" (But, you'll already know that person, because it's *YOU!* Heehee!) You can do this exact exercise in the *MY SOCIAL POWER! WORKBOOK!*

After that, keep that positivity going! The reason we do the seven-day challenge is to let you know how a small action, like writing positive things down on paper and reading them back, can really make you feel incredible. It can change the way you feel about your life and give you more confidence.

INTERESTING TIDBIT:

Write it down! Science has proven that writing things down by hand on paper (not on your phone or computer) but instead, writing it in a journal or notebook boosts your brain's ability to absorb information. It stays in your memory longer and has a stronger impact on how you feel about yourself. This is a time to set your phone to the side. (Eeeek! I know! But those text messages will still be there when you're finished.)

Keep it in your brain-space that your thoughts are **powerful,** so make them positive. *Your inner voice should be your biggest fan, not your biggest critic.* Keep practicing, and soon, you'll see how awesome positive self-talk can be. You've got this!

Tips to Boost Your Mental Health, Body Image and Social Confidence

- **Healthy Habits:** Positive self-talk, eating well, sleeping, and drinking plenty of water are good for your body. They help keep your mind sharp, too.
- **Stay Active:** Exercise isn't just good for your body, it's also great for your brain. It releases chemicals called *endorphins* that make you feel good and happy.
- **Mindful Moments:** Try things like meditation or deep breathing exercises to calm your mind. It's like hitting a pause on your stress.
- **Positive People:** Surround yourself with friends who build you up and make you feel good about yourself. They are like human sunshine!
- **Talk It Out:** When you bottle up your feelings, they can start to feel even bigger. Talking about it with someone you trust can make a huge difference.

Sometimes, you might feel like you can't talk to the people who are closest to you. If that's the case, please ask your parents if a counselor is available to you, or maybe even a therapist or a school guidance counselor. Any way you can talk about it, please do. It's important to get all these feelings out.

Body Language and Building Self-Confidence

Did you know that how you stand, sit, or even smile can totally change how confident you feel? It even changes how other people look at you. Yep, your body language is like a secret weapon for self-confidence. Let's make sure you're using it to your advantage!

- **Stand tall like a superhero:** Shoulders back, chest up, and chin level. Imagine you're wearing an invisible cape, ready to save the day. Standing tall not only makes you look confident, but it helps you *feel* confident, too.
- **Smile... Even if it feels weird:** Smiling sends a signal to your brain that says, "Hey, I'm doing OK!" Plus, smiles are contagious! They make everyone around you feel good, too.
- **Make eye contact:** Looking someone in the eye when you're talking shows that you're interested and sure of yourself. (But don't stare too long! Eeeek! That's awkward!)
- **Watch those fidgety hands:** Try not to twirl your hair, bite your nails, or jiggle your foot too much. Keep your hands still and calm. It shows that you're in control, even if you're a little nervous inside.

EXERCISE TO TRY:

The next time you're walking down the hall, pretend you're a runway model (minus the dramatic poses). Walk tall, swing your arms naturally, and keep your head up. You'll be amazed at how much more confident you'll feel just by walking like you mean it!

Everyday Strategies

- **Be Kind to Yourself:** Treat yourself as nicely as you would treat your friends. No tough talk.
- **Cut Down Screen Time:** Too much screen time can drag down your mood. Give yourself a break and find something fun to do in real life instead!
- **Set Realistic Goals:** Goals that are too big can sometimes seem like too much to tackle, so you might not even try. Listing your goals in a step-by-step format can make your goals more doable.

- **Gratitude Journal:** Take a moment and write down things you're grateful for each day. It can lift your focus from what you don't like to what you love about your life and yourself.
- **Take Action:** Actually go out and do the things you're thinking about and writing about in your journal. Sometimes emotional stress comes because you're not taking action. So, get out there and just go do it!

Even if you're lightning fast on the track team, growing up takes time. Give yourself a break and slow it down. Be patient. To feel good about yourself, it's important to make both your mental and physical health a priority. When your mental health is in a good place, it's easier to see yourself in a positive light. Feeling good mentally can give you the energy to chase your dreams and enjoy life.

As you go through the intricate maze of all these changes, it's really important to have people you can talk to, like your parents, older siblings, or teachers. They can help you understand what's happening and give you support when you need it.

So, take a deep breath… in… out… in… out…

The thrilling journey of becoming your true self is only beginning. Amazing, right?! I'm thrilled for you and your future!

And don't forget, it's okay to ask questions and talk about your feelings. You're not alone. Everyone goes through this growing up phase, and there are a lot of people who can help you along the way. Rock On!

ACTION TAKEAWAYS:

- Practice positive self-talk every day.
- Look in the mirror and say nice things *out loud* to yourself.

- Whenever you think or say something, you're the first person to hear it. Make those thoughts positive and kind!
- Write positive things down on a piece of paper or in a journal. You will keep them in your mind better that way.
- Flip the switch! Decide to be happy and find a better way to deal with your emotions. If something goes wrong, change the script by turning your negative feelings into a positive reaction.
- You can get out of your negative funk by *deciding* to be positive. It's that easy!
- Work on your body language. It's speaking louder than you think.
- Be kind to yourself. You're a work in progress.
- Don't forget: Growing up takes time.
- Please talk to your parents and share your emotions if you're having a difficult time. It's important to include them in the good times, as well. Parents are there to help you when you're down, but they also want to share in your joy and success!
- Emotions can sometimes be exhausting, and sharing them with your parents or an adult you trust can be incredibly helpful.

5. Social Media — Keeping It Cool and Positive

Ever scroll through your feed and think, "Wow, everyone looks so perfect! Their life must be amazing!" Yeah, let's hit the pause button on that one, because guess what? Most of what you see online is a giant illusion.

Almost Everything You See Is FAKE

Spoiler alert: Even the people are sometimes fake (AI generated). Comparing yourself to people on social media is like watching a blooper-free movie and thinking real life works the same way. Double-spoiler alert: It doesn't.

What's Up with the Media?

TV, movies, Instagram, TikTok—they all have their own sneaky little tricks. Let's expose them, shall we?

- **Photoshop Perfection:** This tool can erase zits, shrink waists, and even swap out someone's face! Yikes!

- **Filter Mania:** You know how filters can turn a regular selfie into a supermodel moment? Yeah, that's not real life.
- **Pose Like a Pro:** Ever wonder why *influencers* always look flawless? They spend hours perfecting that "casual" look. Yeah, life is not that casual.
- **Lighting Magic:** The right lighting can make someone look like a glowing goddess. The wrong lighting? Oof. Let's just say we've all seen it.
- **AI Is Here, and It's Wild:** It can literally make up people who don't exist. So yeah, no need to compare yourself to a digital ghost.

How to Be a Media Detective

- **Reality check:** Look at the people around you. Do they look like they walked straight off an Instagram reel? Nope. Because real life isn't edited.
- **Learn the Tricks:** If you know the difference between "filtered" and "authentic," you won't fall for the *fakeness*.
- **Talk About It:** Spread the word! Tell your friends, your family, even your dog (okay, maybe not your dog) that social media is not real life.
- **Why Comparing is the Worst Game Ever:** If you're comparing yourself to people online, you're basically playing a game you can't win. And trust me, it's a game not worth playing.

Most of the time, you're comparing your normal, everyday life to someone else's best, most edited moments. Even your friends might be using apps to tweak their photos. Ever notice how some people's

Social Media — Keeping It Cool and Positive 57

pictures don't quite match how they look in real life? Hmmmm... mystery solved.

When you compare, it steals your joy. It makes you feel bad when, in reality, you're amazing just as you are. So, no more comparing, okay? You've got better things to do.

The FOMO Problem

You know that feeling when you see someone's perfect vacation pictures and suddenly your walk around the neighborhood feels like it sucks rotten eggs? That's FOMO—<u>F</u>ear <u>o</u>f <u>M</u>issing <u>O</u>ut. And social media makes it so much worse.

But guess what? If you're spending all your time scrolling, you're actually missing out on your own life. It's like going to a concert, but only watching it through your phone screen. (I mean, what about the music, man???) You're better than that! Don't get caught up in the trickery, my friend! You're so much better than that fake stuff.

What is Your Goal on Social Media?

Ask yourself:

- Do I want to share cool moments in my life?
- Do I like keeping an online journal?
- Am I looking for fun new ideas?
- Am I here to laugh at funny cat videos?

OR...

- Am I chasing likes and hearts?

Uh-oh. If that last one is it, we need to talk.

Reframing Your Social Media Mindset

Think of your social media page as your personal highlight reel. It's not about impressing people, it's about capturing your own memories.

If you're obsessed with getting likes, you're basically handing over your happiness to a bunch of strangers who may or may not care. (And some of them are only there to *troll* you.) Nope, we are not giving them that power, right?

Keep your power by focusing on what **you** are *doing*. When you care less about how people react and more about what actually makes you happy, you win! And you win BIG!

A Game Plan to Avoid Comparing

- **Focus on You:** Instead of scrolling and stressing, work on your own goals.
- **Keep a "Wins" List:** Write down your *"Wins,"* even the small ones you're proud of. Every little win counts.
- **Screenshot the Good Stuff:** Keep funny, kind, or inspiring messages in a folder. Instant mood booster!
- **Celebrate Your Uniqueness:** You're one of a kind. Own it.
- **Limit Scrolling:** Less time comparing and more time enjoying real life.
- **Turn Comparison Into Motivation:** Instead of feeling bad about someone else's success, think, "Cool! What can I do to grow, too?"
- **Talk About It:** If comparing yourself is making you feel "not

so great," chat with a friend or a trusted adult. They'll remind you how awesome you really are.

Turning Comparisons Into Something Positive

Let's say you see someone who's a rock star at soccer, dancing, or art, and you start feeling kind of down on yourself. Instead of thinking, "Ugh, I'll never be that good," switch it up to:

- "I'd like to learn how to do that!"
- "I'm going to practice a little every day!"
- "I'm inspired, not discouraged!"

PRO TIP: Who's the Coolest Person in the Room?

The coolest person in the room is **not** the one with the most likes, **not** the one with the most *followers*. It's the one who owns their confidence. The person who knows their worth without needing the Internet to tell them, and that can be you!

It all starts with having a super positive attitude. Try to see yourself the way your best friend sees you: Awesome, funny, smart, and real. Let your amazing qualities shine brightly. Focus on all the best parts about yourself, and forget about digging into that negativity drawer for anything else. Stop doubting yourself, okay? Be proud of who you are, even on the days when you don't feel flashy. And trust me, when you feel great about who you are, it totally shows!

Confidence shines way brighter than any Instagram filter.

So hold your head high, stop doubting yourself, and own your awesomeness.

QUOTES:

"I believe in being strong when everything seems to be going wrong. I believe that happy girls are the prettiest girls. I believe that tomorrow is another day, and I believe in miracles." — Audrey Hepburn

"Be yourself; everyone else is already taken." — Oscar Wilde

So go ahead—smile! Believe in miracles, and live your life for you. Because comparing yourself to others? It's a total waste of time!

KEEP YOUR LIFE AMAZING, UNFILTERED, AND 100% REAL!

ACTION TAKEAWAYS:

- Social media is full of *fakeness*. Don't fall for it.
- Stop comparing yourself to someone's edited highlight reel.
- Limit social media time and enjoy your real life.
- Screenshot kind messages and put them in a special folder on your phone to lift your mood later when you need it.
- Set your own goals instead of wishing for someone else's life.
- Focus on what makes you happy, not just what gets likes.
- Find inspiration instead of getting discouraged.
- If you're feeling bad about social media, talk to someone about it.
- Your happiest self is your best self—no filter needed!

6. Tell Those Critics to Take a Hike! (Including the One Inside Your Head)

The world has a big say in how we view ourselves, you know? It's like there's this invisible force that whispers in our ears telling us what's "cool" or "not cool" about how we look. These messages start early, and you see them everywhere. They're in ads and social media, and even in how people talk around us. But first, we need to deal with how we talk to ourselves inside our own heads.

Spotting and Silencing Your Inner Critic

You know that little voice in your head that sometimes whispers mean stuff like, "You're not good enough!" or "Everyone is staring at you because you tripped on the stairs!"? That's your critic. And guess what? It's a total liar.

The first step to shutting it down is spotting it. Here's how:

- **Notice the tone:** Is it super mean or overly dramatic? (Like, "You're the *WORST* dancer ever.") That's not your true voice, that's your inner critic being a bully.
- **Look for exaggerations:** Words like "always," "never," or "everyone," are major red flags that your inner critic bully is alive and well. (Like "You *always* mess up"—Ugh, no you don't!)
- **Pause and question it:** Ask yourself, "Would I ever say this to my best friend?" If the answer is no, it's time to tell that critic to take a hike.
- **Now, here's the fun part:** Replace the critic's voice with a *kind coach voice.* Instead of "You'll never get this right," say, "Hey, everyone starts somewhere, and I'm doing great!" Your inner coach is way cooler, trust me.

Shifting From "What Do *They* Think About Me?" to "What Do *I* Think About Me?"

Raise your hand if you've ever obsessed over what someone else thought about you. (Heck, you better raise both hands!) But here's the deal: Other people's opinions? They're like bubblegum, they are sticky and sometimes annoying, but not worth stressing over.

Instead of worrying about what they think about you, try asking, "What do *I* think about me?" That's a much more important question.

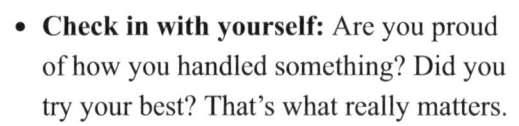

- **Check in with yourself:** Are you proud of how you handled something? Did you try your best? That's what really matters.
- **Be your own hype squad:** Write down three things that you like about yourself. You get bonus points for including something silly like, "I can eat five tacos in one sitting!"

- **Here's a truth:** People are way too busy thinking about their own stuff to spend hours thinking about and judging yours. Seriously, they probably didn't even notice your "bad hair day." So, it's time to let this stuff go!

When you focus on *your* opinion of yourself, you take back your power. Because at the end of the day, **you're the main character in the story of your life,** and the audience is just lucky to be able to watch.

How We See the World

Have you ever noticed how certain body types or styles get all the attention? It's like, if you don't fit in that box, you might start feeling not so great about yourself. Writers and advertisers play a big role in this, too. They are the ones creating these images and messages that can make us feel like we're not good enough unless we look a certain way. It's not cool, but it's real. Things are changing on that, but not quickly enough. It's tough, because at your age, you're still figuring out who you are, right? And then, you've got society throwing all these expectations at you about how you should look and act. It's enough to make anyone feel confused or insecure.

But Here's the Thing

Society's ideas don't have to be the mirror that you view yourself in. These are not requirements. They are not the end-all be-all of how you should see yourself. Your body and mind are yours, unique and outstanding in their own way. While it's okay to be aware of what's out there, don't let it define how you feel about yourself. You're much more than what meets the world's eye, and that's pretty powerful!

Those Around Us

You might have a family member or a friend that seems spectacular to you. Instead of comparing yourself to that person, try using them as a role model.

OR…

Try looking at the differences between you and them. Think about what's lacking in that person's life that you can bring to them.

1. Maybe you have a compassionate way about you that they don't have.
2. Maybe you're an amazing dancer.
3. Maybe you have a great way to do eyeliner they don't know.
4. Maybe you're super funny!

Here's the Deal

<u>Everyone</u>, and I mean everyone, has pluses (+'s) and minuses (-'s).

No one is completely perfect.

No one is completely imperfect.

Everyone is somewhere in the middle.

EVERYONE.

<u>IMPORTANT</u>:

The difference is this: That person you see as being completely spectacular? The reason why they seem so spectacular is that **<u>THEY OWN THEIR PLUSES (+'s)!</u>**

They don't dwell on their minuses (-'s). They don't center their thoughts on negative things like the fact that they might have a zit, or are a little shorter than others, or have a slightly larger nose, or wear older jeans... whatever. My point is, they focus on what makes them shine, not their flaws.

They focus on the fact that they have a super friendly smile, that they are super funny, they are a math whiz, that they can run like a cheetah, or that they are a great drummer.

What they are doing, and they might not even know it is...

They are *"selling"* their strengths to the world, and you, my friend, you are *"buying"* them.

And, that's okay that you buy into their strengths. My point here is, **START *"SELLING"* SOME STRENGTHS OF YOUR OWN!**

GREAT IDEA:

Here's a challenge! Take a moment and list all of your pluses (they are called "attributes") on a separate sheet of paper. Then think to yourself, "How can I show these attributes (+'s) to the world?" What a great time to learn the art of *"Selling Yourself."*

What Does It Mean to Show Off Your Strengths? (*"Selling Yourself"*)

When you show off your strengths, some people (including me) call it *"Selling Yourself."* **It means developing your strengths and showing off the best things about yourself to others.** When you show off your skills, your talents, and your personality, others can see how awesome you are. It's like helping people see why you're super cool and why they should pay attention to you.

PERSONAL SIDE STORY:

When I was about 10 years old, my parents wanted me to learn how to **"sell myself."** That was my Dad's term, and it may be old-fashioned, but it's a great nickname for **showing off your strengths and getting people to like you and believe in you.**

There was this mail order card company and my dad wanted me to go around the neighborhood and sell sets of cards to people to build my confidence and to learn the art of *"Selling Myself."*

He said, "Let's make this a competition! I will sell some at work and you sell them around the neighborhood. Whoever wins after one month gets this crisp $20 bill!" Then he waved that $20 bill around in front of my face. My eyes followed it back-and-forth. "But first, you need to practice." And I'm thinking, *$20 bucks? Now you're talking!* But, practice? I need to practice *what*, exactly?

They put me behind the laundry room door and made me knock on the door, pretending like I was knocking on the door of the neighborhood customer. (Knock, knock, knock) Then I fumbled through some mumbly-mouthed "Uh… well... wanna buy some cards?" And they said, "Nope! Not good enough. You need to introduce yourself and tell them your name. Tell them that you live in the neighborhood. Maybe even point out our house. Then tell about what you're selling, why you're selling it, and why they should buy from you." *Geez, that sounds like an awful lot of things to say.* So, we practiced and practiced (and practiced and practiced!) until after a while, I started having fun with it. Later that night, I went to my room, I wrote the goal down and taped it to my bathroom mirror. This was happening!

The next day, it was finally time to start knocking on doors outside of my laundry room. The first house I went to, boy, I was so nervous. But after my "Sell Myself Introduction," the woman that answered the door actually bought one box! Then I thought, *Wow! This "selling yourself" stuff really works!* The more I did it, the better I got at it.

Every day, my Dad would come home giggling about how many boxes he sold. At first, it made me angry. It felt like he was cheating because he got to sell to all these people he already knew. He didn't really have to "sell himself" to *anybody*, but I had to "sell myself" to *everybody*. It didn't seem fair. But pretty quickly, that anger got me super motivated because I wanted to beat him at this sales game! Frankly, I wanted to *destroy* him! Hahaha! Once I knew I could actually sell, I not only *wanted* to get that $20, I *NEEDED* TO GET THAT $20! I knew I needed to set my goal high to beat him. So, I told myself I wouldn't stop until I reached $100+ in commissions. (Yikes! That's a lot!) After that, every day when I got home, I added up my sales and figured out my commissions. To be honest, I was turning into a card-selling wizard!

One day, I complained to him that I was only getting one or two sales per house. He said, "Well then, have a 'Special Sale!'" *A special sale?* He said, "Tell them, 'Today we're having a Special Sale! For every 10 things you buy, you get one of these (pointing to the cheapest card sets) for FREE!'" I said, "But Dad, the company is not having a "Special Sale!" I would have to pay for them!" He said, "Yes, but you'll make more sales in the long run. You'll make more money by selling more products, and people will love you because they're getting a *deal!* Everybody loves a deal! Do the math, you'll see I'm right."

So, I did the math, and yes, was he right! I got 20% commissions off the top from the card company. Even if somebody bought 10 of the cheapest card sets, I'd still be making $1.00 per house. But here's the thing: Everybody *hated buying* those cheap card sets, but everybody *loved getting* them for free! My Dad was a genius! I went back to the houses that bought from me and gave them credit for their previous purchases to go toward the "Special Sale!" Almost every single one of them upped their purchases to participate in the new deal! My commission was at least $4.00, and some were as high as $10 per house!

When that 30th day came around, my Dad sheepishly pulled out his list of sales, feeling bad that he totally creamed me. You see, neither one of us shared our ongoing totals. It was all completely secret. But he was wrong! I outsold him two-to-one, doubling his number of sales!! Both my parents were shocked and amazed, and so completely proud of me. I wouldn't change that moment for the world. Not only did I win that crisp $20 bill, I also earned $101 in commissions! But moreover, I earned the respect of my Dad and Mom. Learning to "sell myself" was really one of the best gifts my parents ever gave me.

And hmmm… and **$121?!** Not too shabby for a 10-year-old kid!!

VERY IMPORTANT:

It's important that you know that **I AM NOT TELLING YOU TO GO OUT AND SELL THINGS DOOR-TO-DOOR.** This story happened during a different time than it is now. But it is important that you, along with your parents, come up with a game plan (along with exercises like "Behind the Laundry Room Door" technique) to help you build your self-confidence and your emotional strength so that you can *"sell yourself"* in life.

Doing things like this with other people (like practicing *"selling yourself"* with your Mom and Dad) is called "role playing." It's called that because you're literally playing a role (like a part in a play) until you get the techniques down and make them your own. Once you get them down, you're no longer playing a role, you're actually *living* the technique.

It's important to practice the words that you're going to say out loud, so that when you're in a real-life situation, your words just roll effortlessly right out of your mouth.

Role playing is a pretty powerful tool that people of all ages use. It puts you on the spot in front of another person, it makes you think on your feet, and it forces you to communicate with your words. When you get this down, your nerves will simply float away because you'll feel confident in what you're saying and then you'll be unstoppable!

Let's Start *"Selling Yourself!"* Now! Let's Start Showing Off Those Great Qualities You Have!

Be Your Own Cheerleader! Be the hype squad for your own great strengths. When you put the spotlight on your uniquely outstanding qualities and start *"selling yourself"* to others, those other things you think are not so great will get smaller and smaller in your thoughts. And, at some point, you probably won't even think about them much at all. Cool, right?!

So, get out there!

Start *selling* your strengths!

Start *selling* your pluses (+'s)!

Start *"Selling Yourself!"*

The world is just waiting for your own special magic!

ACTION TAKEAWAYS:

- Don't let society tell you how to feel about yourself.
- No one is perfect.

- Figure out some of your strengths and start *"selling"* them to the world!
- Master the art of *"Selling Yourself." "Sell"* your strengths, your talents, your ideas, your pluses (+'s)!
- Practice what you're going to say out loud with another person (role-playing) so that by the time you say it in real life, your words just roll right off your tongue. Easy-peasy!
- Be your own hype squad!
- Got questions? Talk it out with your parents or a trusted adult.

7. The Power of Setting Goals!

Let's talk about something super important that can help you get the most out of your life now, and in the future: **GOALS!** Think of goals as your own personal superpowers. They help you focus your energy and make amazing things happen.

Why Are Goals Important?

Goals are like a road map for you to achieve your dreams. They show you where you want to go and help you get there. Whether it's acing a test, learning a new skill, or being kinder to others, having a goal gives you direction and purpose. It's like having a treasure map, but instead of gold, you're finding your own greatness!

How to Choose a Goal

Choosing a goal is like picking a fun adventure. Here's how to do it:

- **Dream Big:** Think about what motivates you or what you've always wanted to do. It could be anything from learning to play an instrument to even becoming a pro athlete.
- **Be Specific:** Instead of saying, "I want to be better at math," focus on "I'm going to work to get an 'A' on my next math test." This way, you know exactly what you're aiming for.
- **Make It Realistic:** While dreaming big is great, make sure your goal is something you can actually achieve with a bit of hard work. If you're just starting out in basketball, maybe aim to make a certain number of baskets rather than becoming the MVP right away.

How to Go After Your Goal

Okay, you've picked your goal. Now what? Time to go after it like a superhero!

- **Write It Down on Paper:** Writing your goal down on paper helps you remember it better. Then post it somewhere you will look at it every day, like on the mirror in your bathroom or bedroom. Seeing your goal visually will help cement it in your mind.
- **Break It Down:** Big goals can seem scary, so break them into smaller steps. If your goal is to read a big book, start with reading a few pages each day.
- **Create a Plan:** Decide what you need to do each day or week to get closer to your goal. Write it down or make a cool checklist.
- **Get Creative:** Think of different ways you can accomplish your goal. This is called *brainstorming*!
- **Set a Deadline:** Setting a deadline requires you to perform *pronto!* It means that your goal won't go on forever, because you will have many goals that you'll want to achieve in life.

- **Make it Public!** By telling others about your goal, it keeps you wanting to achieve that goal. Making your goal public creates a sense of, "Everybody knows what I'm doing, so I better get out there and do it!"
- **Stay Positive:** Believe in yourself! Every superhero faces challenges, but they don't give up!

How to Stay Focused

Staying focused can be tough, but here are some tricks to help you out:

- **Remind Yourself:** Write your goal on a sticky note or piece of paper. Put it where you can see it every day, like your bathroom mirror. This helps you remember why you started your goal.
- **Celebrate Small Wins:** Every time you complete a step towards your goal, celebrate it! It could be a happy dance, a yummy treat, or just a high-five with a friend.
- **Avoid Distractions:** If something is taking your attention away from your goal, like too much screen time, try to limit it. Keep your eyes on the prize.

What To Do When You Achieve Your Goal

You did it! You've reached your goal! Now, what's next?

- **Celebrate Big:** You worked hard, so give yourself a big pat on the back. Maybe even have a mini party to share your success with your friends and family.
- **Look Back On How You Did It:** Think about what you learned and how you felt achieving your goal. This is called "reflection." When we look back on how we did things, it

helps us prepare to do it better the next time in a similar situation. When you analyze the process, it helps you grow even more.
- **Set a New Goal:** Don't stop now! Pick a new goal and start the adventure all over again. The best part about goals? There's always a new one waiting; something new and next-level exciting to achieve!

IMPORTANT INSIGHT ABOUT THE POWER OF REFLECTION:

So, you finally crushed that goal you set. Whether it was acing that math test, mastering a new trick on your skateboard, or sticking to a fitness routine—You did it! High five! But before you move on to the next big thing, it's super important to take a minute and think about how you got there.

Reflecting back on your goals isn't only about patting yourself on the back (though you totally should). It's about digging deeper and figuring out what worked, what didn't work, and what you learned about yourself along the way. Maybe you discovered you've got more grit than you thought, or maybe you realized there was a smarter, faster way to reach your goals next time.

Reflection is like looking at a map after a long road trip. You'll see the twists and turns you took, and that helps you plan for an even better route next time. Did you hit some bumps along the way? Great! Those bumps are where you probably learned the most. Maybe you figured out that you actually love working out early in the morning, or that you're better at staying focused when you take breaks. Or maybe you realized you needed to ask for help sooner instead of trying to do everything on your own.

When you take time to reflect, you unlock a new level of self-awareness. It's like discovering a secret power you didn't know you had.

The Power of Setting Goals! 75

You'll start to see patterns in how you work, then you can tweak your approach for the next goal. It feels pretty awesome to look back and see how far you've come.

So, yeah, smashing your goals is epic, but reflecting on them? That's where the real magic happens. It's how you turn today's win into tomorrow's success story.

PERSONAL SIDE STORY:

Let's think back to the last chapter about "Tell Those Critics to Take a Hike! (Including the One Inside Your Head)."

Remember the story I was just telling you about selling cards door-to-door? That was my personal story about *"selling myself,"* but after reflecting on it, that story is also about setting goals!

- In the beginning, there was only **ONE GOAL** (to learn how to "sell myself" and gain confidence by selling card sets door-to-door).
- It became a **REALISTIC GOAL** after my parents role-played with me and taught me how to sell cards in my neighborhood by first practicing behind the "laundry room door."
- My parents had me **BREAK IT DOWN** when they suggested I introduce myself, tell the *what, when, why,* and *how* I was selling cards in the neighborhood. But after further thought and being more **SPECIFIC** about my goal, there were a few other goals that developed in this story.
- **MAIN GOAL:** To learn how to successfully "sell myself" to others and build my confidence.
- Once I knew I had the skill to sell these cards, these three other specific goals came into focus:
- **SPECIFIC GOAL #1**: Beat my Dad in sales.
- **SPECIFIC GOAL #2:** Win that $20 bill.

- **SPECIFIC GOAL #3:** Once I figured out I could actually sell those cards, I decided to **DREAM BIG** and make the goal of getting at least $100 in commissions.
- **SET A DEADLINE:** My Dad set the deadline of 30 days.
- **MAKE IT PUBLIC:** I was out there selling door to door! Can't get much more public than that! Plus, both of my parents knew, along with a couple of my friends. Them knowing that I was out there selling cards made me feel like I had to achieve it!
- **STAY POSITIVE:** I really believed that I could obtain that $100 commission goal, and I cheered myself on every day to achieve that goal.
- There were different things that I had to do to achieve my goals. I knew I wasn't going to be able to sell that many cards to just the four houses surrounding my home. I was going to have to **CREATE A PLAN** and **GET CREATIVE:** First I would have to:
- **BREAK IT DOWN #1:** Branch out to a wider sales area.
- **BREAK IT DOWN #2:** Keep a list of the houses that were not home when I went by the first time.
- **BREAK IT DOWN #3:** (This was Getting Creative) Knock on doors that were unsure about a purchase the first time and try again to get them to buy.
- **BREAK IT DOWN #4:** (This was Getting Creative) Resell prior purchases with the new "It's on Special Sale!" technique.
- **REMIND MYSELF:** My Dad helped to remind me of my goal by giving me little digs, which he knew would irritate me and push me to work harder.
- **CELEBRATED SMALL WINS #1:** By counting up my sales each night and doing a happy-dance in my room.
- **CELEBRATED SMALL WINS #2:** By counting up my commissions each night. Double happy dance!
- **AVOID DISTRACTION:** I knew there were only so many hours in a day, and I only had 30 days to accomplish my goals. So…

The Power of Setting Goals!

1. I did my homework first.
2. I sold until sundown.
3. Then ate dinner.
4. Then showered.
5. Tallied my sales.
6. If there was any time left, I watched TV.

- **Now keep in mind,** my parents didn't teach me anything outside the "laundry room door sales crash course" and the "Make a Special Sale" technique. Somehow, all those other steps I figured out myself. Plus, my parents didn't tell me to go back out and re-sell my prior purchases with the new "It's on Special Sale!" approach. Somehow, I *knew* I had to do it. Heck, I was in a competition with my Dad! I *HAD* to figure out new ways to reach my goal. So, I had to use my creative powers to figure out how I was going to make more sales in order to beat him. I had to figure things out on my own.
- My point here is: **You will discover great things about yourself** and you will create new techniques that will help you achieve your goal. When you **get creative,** you will surprise yourself over and over, and those surprises will be powerful! You will say to yourself, **"Wow! I did this!!"** If I could do it, then you can do it, too!
- **CELEBRATE BIG:** I got to celebrate big by going out to my favorite Mexican restaurant for tacos and sopapillas drenched in honey (Super Yum!) Plus, I was finally able to buy that awesome thing I'd been dreaming about—a giant lime green bean bag chair! My first precious victory of many!
- **SET NEXT GOAL:** Straight A's!!

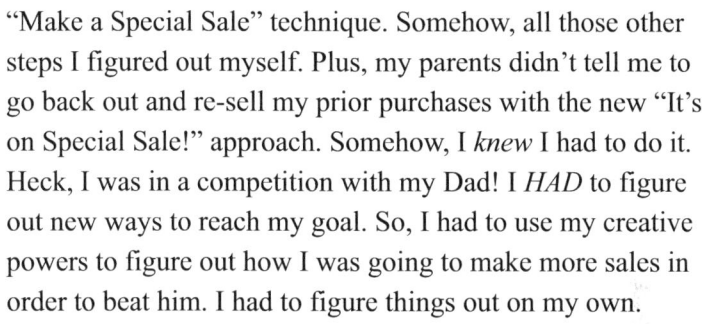

Goals are your secret weapon to becoming the best version of yourself. They guide you, keep you focused, and help you grow. You've got the power to achieve anything you set your mind to. So, dream big, stay focused, and keep reaching for the stars. You're amazing and your journey is only beginning!

Let's go, superstar! Your goals are waiting!

ACTION TAKEAWAYS:

- Goals are like a map of your dreams.
- How to Choose a Goal: 1. Dream big. 2. Be specific. 3. Make it realistic.
- How to Go After Your Goal: 1. Break it down. 2. Create a plan. 3. Get creative. 4. Stay positive. 5. Make it public.
- How to Stay Focused: 1. Remind yourself. 2. Celebrate small wins. 3. Avoid distractions.
- When You Achieve Your Goal: 1. Celebrate big. 2. Use reflection to look back on what you did. 3. Set a new goal.
- Don't forget to get your copy of the **MY SOCIAL POWER! WORKBOOK** It's packed full of interesting and fun ideas and exercises to help you achieve all the goals your heart desires!
- You will discover things about yourself and create new techniques that will help you achieve your goal. You will surprise yourself! Over and over, those surprises will be powerful! You can do more than you think!
- Don't be afraid to get creative.
- Talk with other people (like your parents, mentors, coaches, or trusted adults) to help you achieve all the goals you want to go for! By including important people whom you respect in your goal-setting, it's a reliable way to help you accomplish your goals faster!

8. Everything In Life is Choices

Choices are Everywhere… Choose Wisely!

Here's the scoop: Life is like a mega-mall of choices. Every day, from the moment you wake up to when you hit the sack, you're making choices. What you wear, what you eat, how to spend your time—choices, choices, choices! And guess what? Just like choosing your coolest clothes, the choices you make can totally change your day, and even your life!

Why Choices Matter

- **Choices Show You Who You Are:** Choosing to be kind when you could be mean says a lot about you. Or, choosing to share your snacks or help a friend with their project can make someone's day.

- **Choices Shape Your Future:** Are you doing your homework or slacking off? Each choice can lead to totally different paths.

Smart Choice Tips

Tip 1: Think Before You Choose

Before you decide on something big, take a pause. Think it out. Think about what could happen after you make that choice. It's like looking both ways before you cross the street. You don't want your choice to run you over, do you? No, you want it to lift you up and make your life better!

Tip 2: Ask for Advice

Sometimes deciding on your own is tough. It's cool to ask others what they think. Chat with your parents, your older sibling, or even your best bud.

Tip 3: Go with Your Gut

You know that funny feeling you get when something feels right or wrong? That's your gut talking to you. It's also known as *intuition*. Listen to it! It's your "spidey-sense," and often knows what's up before you do.

Sometimes, a good question to ask before doing something is, "Would I want my grandma to know that I am doing this?" That doesn't work for everything, but it does work a lot of the time to help you realize whether a decision might be a good one or a bad one.

Tip 4: Weigh the Pros and Cons (Pluses +'s and Minuses -'s)

Sometimes, it helps to write down the good points and the bad points of each choice. Like, if you're deciding whether to join the soccer team or the drama club, list what's cool and what's not so cool about each. Making a list on a sheet of paper helps you figure out what the good things and the not-so-good things are about a decision. It's a very useful tool, and some people use it their entire lives.

Tip 5: Give Yourself Time

Don't rush your decisions, especially the big ones. Anything that requires a rushed decision or if someone is pressuring you for an answer will most likely have a crummy outcome. If you can, sleep on it. You might see things differently in the morning.

Tip 6: Put Yourself First

Make sure you're making this decision for you, that you're doing this for the right reasons, and not to please someone else. Sometimes, when we try to please others, it clouds our judgment. You need to take care of #1. You've got to take care of YOU!

Tip 7: Choose to Be Amazing!

All of life is a choice, so choose to be amazing!

Everyday Choices That Rock!

- **Choose to Smile:** Even if you're not feeling 100%, smiling can trick your brain into feeling a bit happier. Plus, it's contagious!
- **Choose to Move:** Whether it's doing 10 jumping jacks or dancing around in your room, moving makes you feel awesome and energized.
- **Choose to Be Positive:** When stuff goes wrong, like bombing a quiz, try to find the good side. Make it a chance to learn something new!
- **Choose to Try New Things:** Maybe it's trying a new food or picking up a new hobby. New experiences open up so many

doors. You'll discover things you didn't know you could fall in love with.

What Happens If You Choose Wrong?

Hey, nobody's perfect. Sometimes we make choices that are, "Oops!"—not so great. Here's the best part—you can make another choice to fix things. Apologize if you hurt someone, try again if you failed, and learn from what happened. It's all about growing up and getting better.

PERSONAL INSIGHT:

My grandpa used to say, "Show me your friends, and I'll show you who you are." This means your friends are probably just like you. Looking at your friends is like looking in a mirror.

- When you look at your friends, do you like what you see?
- If your parents looked at your friends, would they be proud of how they act?
- When you look at your friends, do you ask, "Is this who I want to be?"

Hopefully, you say, "Yes! I love my friends. I love who they are. I love how they act. I love how they add a positive statement to the world."

But, maybe you look at them and see a lot of "No, I don't like what they do. I don't want to be like them." Then, in that case, you'll need to take a hard look at yourself. You'll need to make some tough choices and change your friendship groups.

Because, make no mistake, choosing your friends is also a choice. Make sure that you're choosing friends who add quality to your life.

- If you choose good people, you're probably a good person doing good things.

OR...

- If you choose people who do negative things, you might be going down the wrong path.

Certain choices, including choices of friends, can change our lives. Let me repeat that:

Choices of friends can change our lives.

So, be picky! You're worth it!

What If I Can't Decide?

Know that not making a decision is actually a decision, and it's normally not a good one.

By not making a decision and by not choosing your outcome, you're letting fate, chance, or other people who might not have your best interests in mind choose for you. Remember: Your choices matter. Make choices that feel true to YOU.

Don't let the power of choice be taken away from you!

Instead, go through Tips 1-7 (above) and figure it out.

1. Think before you choose.
2. Ask for advice.
3. Go with your gut.
4. Weigh the pros and cons.
5. Give yourself time.
6. Put yourself first.
7. Choose to be amazing!

Every choice you make builds a part of the awesome person you're becoming. Think about what you want to be known for and make choices that lead you there. You've got this!

Look Back on Your Choices

At the end of the day, take a moment to think about the choices you made.

- What worked well?
- What could you have done better?

Figuring these things out helps you make smarter decisions the next time.

Keep a Decision Journal

Why not keep a journal about your decisions? Write down the big decisions, tell how you felt about them, and what the outcomes were. Over time, you will see how much you've learned and grown from all these great decisions.

Keep choosing what feels right and watch how powerful you can become! It's all about using your decision-making power to create the awesome person you're meant to be in this world. Keep it up, superstar!

ACTION TAKEAWAYS:

- Choices matter.
- When making a decision, go through the 7 Smart Choice Tips: 1. Think before acting on it. 2. Ask for advice. 3. Go with your gut. 4. Weigh the pros and cons. 5. Give yourself time. 6. Put yourself first. 7. Choose to be amazing!
- If you choose poorly, you can always choose again.
- Take a look at your friendship groups and ask, "Do I like what I see?"

- Choices in friendships can change your life. Be picky! You're worth it!
- Keep a decision journal, like in the ***MY SOCIAL POWER! WORKBOOK.***
- Reflection: Look back on what worked or didn't work.
- Let your parents help guide you in your decision-making. With a great conversation, they can offer excellent viewpoints or ideas on how to help you make the right choice. So chat with your parents, a trusted adult, an older sibling, or even your best friend. Get the advice you need!

9. Make a Difference with Your Review

Remember that wild moment when you realized, "Whoa! I'm growing up?" Your body was changing and your future was around the corner. It was a mashup of "Yikes, this is new!" and "Wow, this is so awesome!" And then you got that clueless, "Wait, I'm going to be an *adult*???" feeling?

Just like you needed advice, other teens need the same. **You** can be the one who makes them feel less alone, less confused, and way more confident.

Helping others makes you feel like a total superhero. People who lift others up live happier lives, so why not share that energy everywhere?

If we have the chance to help ourselves **and** lift someone else up at the same time—well, heck—I think we should try.

Would you spend 60 seconds to make someone's life a little brighter?

1. **Tap the link or scan the QR code**.

https://dub.sh/AQQA

2. **Share your feelings**. How did this book help you? Did it make you smile? Did you have an "Oh, I get it now!" moment?

3. Give your **Written Review, Your Stars** ★★★★★ **Rating, and Submit**, and know that you just helped someone else improve their life in the coolest way possible.

4. **Maybe add a picture or video** of yourself to your review and online talking about how the book helped you! I'd love to see who you are! **#MySocialPower!**

It feels good to share the secret sauce of growing up! So, why not be that person?

That's it! Your words could totally change someone's life. How cool is that? Thank you for being a part of this mission to spread confidence, kindness, and a whole lot of social power!

Confidence shared is confidence multiplied. Keep shining, superstar!

Your biggest fan,

SheriBelle

10. The Mystery of Mean Girls (And Bullies)

Have you ever wondered why some girls at school can be, well, uh, not so nice? It's like one minute you're all giggling together about a funny meme and the next, you might find yourself on the not-so-fun side of a mean comment. Girls are supposed to be your sisterhood, your compadres, right? So, why can't we all stick together? It's confusing, I know.

If you're a guy reading this book, you might want to continue reading just to figure out a little bit more about girls.

Well, buckle up because we're going to study the world of "mean girls" and try to figure out what makes them tick. Don't worry, we're going to try to keep it light and fun, even though the topic can be a bit thorny.

Why Are Some Girls (And Bullies) Mean?

Here's the scoop: Think of it like playing a video game where everyone tries to score the most points to win. Some people think that by putting other people down, they will score big points and feel better about themselves. Mean girls and bullies are often like magicians putting on a show. They pull out the mean tricks to distract everyone (including themselves) from their own insecurities.

Yep, you heard that right. Sometimes, people act mean because they're feeling unsure or scared inside. They might have a tough home life where they feel ignored or unseen. Maybe they live in an abusive situation, or maybe they have a sibling that takes up the entire spotlight. They might struggle with their own body image and feel pressure to be perfect. So, they put on their "mean girl or bully mask" to hide what's really going on. Or, they might just be trying to climb the social ladder at school and think being tough will get them to the top.

The problem is, this mean behavior doesn't actually make them feel good for very long. Since the excitement they get is short-lived, they do it again and again to get the same thrill. It's a nasty cycle. Don't let yourself play a part in that cycle. You can stop the game. More on that later…

Queen Bees and Wannabees

First, there's usually a "queen bee" in the mix. That's the girl who's like the director of the group. She is the one who calls all the shots and the others in her group are her followers.

- **The Copycat Crew:** You'll see that the queen bee has sidekicks or what I like to call the "copycat crew." They are the girls who tag along with the queen bee because it feels safer and cooler than being on their own. They might mimic mean behavior to fit in or because they're scared of becoming the "queen bee's" next target. It's like a game of follow the leader, but the game isn't very nice.

- **Spotlight Stealers:** Mean girls and bullies are like spotlight stealers in the talent show. They want all eyes on them. They crave attention and might use gossip or teasing to keep the spotlight shining brightly on them. When everyone is talking about the drama they've created, they're soaking up the attention like a sponge.
- **The Jealous Jellies:** And let's not forget about the jealous bullies. Sometimes, bullies and mean girls act mean because they're jealous of what someone has or what someone can do. Maybe it's your awesome new backpack, your knack for getting A's, or that you're super chill and everyone likes hanging out with you. Their jealousy makes them act like they just sucked on a lemon—sour and bitter.
- **The Boredom Bunch:** Believe it or not, some bullies throw out trouble because they're just... bored. (Really?) Yep, you heard that right. When there's not enough excitement in their lives, they create drama because it's something to do. It's like if you poke a sleeping cat just to see if it will jump. Yeah, not so nice.
- **Insecurity, Inc.:** At the heart of it all, many mean girls and bullies are simply dealing with their own struggles. They might feel bad about themselves and think that by making other people feel small, it will make them feel bigger. It's like trying to build the tallest building by knocking down all the others around it.

Mean Girls:

So now you see that they exist. They're real. They're confusing. And sometimes they act like the entire school is their runway, their throne room, and drama stage all rolled into one.

But here's the twist: Most of the time? It's not even about you. It's about control, attention, insecurity, or weird group rules nobody voted for.

What Is a Mean Girl Anyway?

A mean girl is not someone who's having a bad day. She's not someone who's direct or confident or speaks her mind, because just so you know, being assertive does not equal being mean.

A Mean Girl is Someone Who:

- Excludes on purpose ("You can't sit with us.")
- Gossips and spreads rumors to hurt people.
- Gives the "silent treatment" like it's a punishment.
- Rolls her eyes like it's an Olympic sport.
- Acts nice to your face, but destroys you behind your back.
- Makes you feel like you're always walking on eggshells.
- Sometimes she'll smile at you while she's being cruel. That is next-level confusing.

The Sugar-Coated Group

Mean girl groups don't always look mean. They might wear matching bracelets. They might plan parties and post pics with #besties. They might even give hugs and compliments like: "You're so pretty—I wish I could pull off *that* outfit." (Translation: "That outfit's *weird* and you shouldn't wear it.") **They are meanness, in lip gloss.**

- When you're **NOT IN** the group? You feel it. Left out. Invisible. Like you missed the invite to some secret club.
- And when you're **IN** the group? You might feel like you have to follow the queen bee or risk being the next target.

"Is It Me? Or Is This Friendship… Kind of Toxic?"

If your friend group:

- Makes you feel anxious about every text
- Gossips about each other nonstop
- Punishes you for spending time with other people
- Controls what you wear or say
- Makes you feel like you have to shrink to fit in

That's not a friendship. You deserve people who:

- Cheer you on
- Let you be weird
- Don't make you pick sides
- Have your back

Let's Check Your Friendships…

1. Write down the names of three people in your friendship group.
2. Next to each name, write down one word that describes how they make you feel.
3. Then ask yourself: "Do I feel safe, seen, and celebrated with this person?"

Hmmm… did you get any insight from this friendship check? Do you see *Red Flags* or *Green Flags?*

REAL TALK REMINDER:

- You don't have to shrink to fit into any friendship.
- Your real friends won't ask you to change, hide, or hurt others to stay in the group.

- Friendship is supposed to make you feel good about yourself. Full stop.

So What Can You Do?

1. Don't play the game. You don't have to return the glare, or roast them back, or make someone else feel bad just to fit in. That's *their* playbook, not yours.

2. Find your real friends. Your people are out there. The ones that laugh at your jokes, support your projects, and don't get jealous when you win. They may not be the loudest crew, but they'll be the most loyal.

3. Say NO to meanness. You can say: "I'm not into gossip," or "That felt kind of harsh," or "Can we not do this?" You don't have to yell or go full drama queen. So, speak up. Set the tone. And protect yourself.

4. Talk to someone you trust. If the group is really messing with your confidence? Talk to someone like a counselor, a coach, an auntie, or your cool older cousin. You're not "being dramatic." You're taking care of your heart.

5. Stay powerful. Mean girls lose their sparkle when you stop giving them your shine. The most powerful thing you can do? Keep being you. Live it out loud. With kindness. With boundaries. And with serious confidence.

BIG TIP:

You don't need a permission slip to exist. And you definitely don't need to change who you are just to be a part of someone else's group. You don't need a group that makes you *prove yourself.* You need a group that makes you *feel like yourself.*

You're Not Too Much

Let them call you "extra." Let them *side-eye* your outfit. Let them say whatever they want. And you? You keep rising. Because here's the secret: Mean girl energy is loud. But kindness? Kindness is **LEGENDARY.**

ACTION TAKEAWAYS:

- In a mean girl group, there is a queen bee and her copycat crew.
- You don't have to join the mean girl game.
- Choose friends who make you feel safe being YOU.
- Don't be the back-up bully.
- Don't join the mean girl group. Your shine is bigger than that.
- Find your real friends. Create your own circle.
- It's important that you talk to a trusted adult (like your parents) when you're having to deal with a mean girl (or a mean guy, or a bully, or a cyberbully) situation. Even if you just need to vent, these things are often hard to handle on your own.

11. "Dude, What's Up With These Mean Friendships?" (AKA, Mean Boys Are Real)

Okay, so this one's for the guys out there (and honestly, anyone who's ever wondered what's up with friendships).

So even if you're a girl reading this chapter, you might want to take a look at this chapter to understand guys a little better.

Let Me Set You Straight:

Guys have their own version of drama, oh yeah. They might not do the eye rolls, and the whisper triangles like some girls do (well, some of them might). But trust me, they've got their own brand of social weirdness. It's just sneakier. Quieter. Sometimes… sweatier? Hahaha!

Or maybe they just hide it better… or worse? But, *"guy drama"* comes in weird actions—like dodgeballs to the face, awkward group chats, and mysterious lunch table betrayals.

It's tough. No doubt about it.

But Why Are Some Guys (and Bullies) So Mean?

Okay, so you're minding your own business, being your awesome self—and BOOM!—someone comes in hot with a mean joke, a shove, or a seriously rude comment.

And you're like, **"Bro. What did I even do?"**

Here's the Truth Bomb:

It's usually not about you. It's about them.

Yep. Plot twist, am I right? When someone acts mean or bully-ish, it's usually because:

- They feel small and want to feel big.
- They don't know how to deal with their own stress or embarrassment.
- They're scared of being made fun of, so they do it first.
- They think being loud equals being powerful.
- Or… They've got stuff going on that nobody else sees.
- They're dealing with hormones that are new and they don't understand.
- They're dealing with body changes that feel awkward; like getting taller from growth spurts (or not getting taller)
- Or sadly, they're just bored.

It's like their emotions are like a soda can they shook up—instead of opening it gently, they just *explode it on everyone around them.*

But Here's the Key:

You do NOT have to stand there and take the fizz to the face.

You can:

- Walk away like the legend you are.
- Say, "Not cool, man" (if you feel safe to do so).
- Talk to someone who gets it (a coach, a teacher, your cool aunt, whoever).

So, Are You Ready? Let's break it down.

Exhibit A: The Silent Unfriend

You ever have a bro just… vanish?

- Monday, you're building a whole video game world together.
- Tuesday, he's laughing at your jokes.
- Wednesday, he's hanging with a *different* crew and acting like you don't exist. No note. No "we need to talk." No goodbye message written in ketchup on a napkin.

Just—**poof**.

And here's the thing: A lot of guys are TERRIFIED of saying, "Hey man, I'm kind of upset about this."

So instead, what does that wounded person do? They just go silent. They sit somewhere else. They act like they're busy when they're not. They're in this weird state of not knowing what's going on with their old friend, and sitting there scratching their head asking, "Where did my friend go?"

Story Time:

> So imagine this: Joe and his best bud, Lucas, play the same video game every day after school. They're basically the kings

of the computer screen. And then one day, Lucas stops joining Joe's game. He doesn't text. Doesn't wave. And at lunch? Sits with someone else. (WHAAAAT?)

Does Joe ask him what's up? No. Does he cry in his spaghetti? Maybe a little—but mostly, Joe just acts like he doesn't care. (But, he totally cares.) The end.

Guys are sometimes weird about emotions. (Girls are too!) It's like we think saying "That hurts my feelings" will cause us to explode into a puff of emotional smoke.

So, as you can see in that story, guys sort of think emotions are like lava. You know that game, "The Floor is Lava"? Except this time the lava is emotion, and generally guys leap to avoid that. (Spoiler Alert: You won't melt.) You might even make a real friendship stronger by being honest, by stepping in that lava, and having a real conversation about it.

Wild, I know.

It takes bravery.

Yup.

Difficult? Yeah, it's tough.

Exhibit B: Mr. I'm-Too-Cool-Now

You know this guy. The one who used to like the same goofy stuff you did—fart jokes and weird YouTube videos, but now suddenly he acts like he's applying to Harvard?

He says things like:

- That game is for kids.
- You still do *that*?
- Nah, I don't play *that* anymore. I've moved on.

You're like, "BRO. You're a teenager. What are you, a retired CEO now?"

Truth is, some boys try to grow up too fast. When they feel awkward or unsure, instead of being real, they act superior. They pretend they're "above" the fun stuff. But really? They just don't want to look uncool in front of someone else.

But Newsflash: Confidence isn't about ditching what you love. It's about **loving it louder**.

Exhibit C: The Roast Master General

Okay, now we get to the "*funny guy.*" The class clown. The guy who always has a joke. And yeah, he's hilarious until the jokes are always about **YOU**.

- "Nice haircut. Did you use a lawnmower?"
- "Wow, those shoes! Did your grandma pick those out?"
- "What kind of name is that? Sounds like a sneeze."
- "Hey, don't pick him. He's only good at losing!"

At first, you laugh along. You don't want to seem lame, or that you "can't take a joke." But eventually? You start wondering if everyone's laughing ***with*** you… or are they laughing ***at*** you?

Big difference.

Here's the deal: **Being a funny guy doesn't mean that you have to be a *mean* guy**. If the joke only makes one person laugh and makes another person feel like poop, it's not a joke. It's just bullying in a clown costume.

You don't have to roast people to be funny. And if your so-called friend can't be hilarious without hurting people, then maybe he's not that funny (or that great of a friend) after all.

Exhibit D: The Jealous Bro

This one is sneaky. You get a new friend. You're hanging out with your old friend, but also with your new friend. And your original friend goes into full mystery mode.

- Stops talking to you.
- Makes sarcastic jokes about your new friend.
- Starts *competing* like it's the Friendship Olympics.

Suddenly, he reacts with, "Oh, so now *he's* your best friend? I guess you don't care about playing video games anymore. You probably even make slime hearts together."

Jealousy? Yeah, boys get it too. They just don't say it. They act like it's not happening, and instead, they sabotage what still could've been a good friendship.

Here's a tip: If you're feeling left out, say something. If your friend is acting weird, question him about it. Don't let the bro codes stop you from being real, and don't let it stop you from keeping a good friend.

Exhibit E: The "You Can't Sit with Us" Guy Group

Boys have cliques, too. They might not have matching scrunchies or choreographed hallway dances (Okay, some of them do), but don't be fooled—they've got their own

"Dude, What's Up With These Mean Friendships?" (AKA, ...

squads. Some are good, some are not so good. It all depends on how they treat you.

IMPORTANT NOTE: Every group is different. Some of these guys are the coolest humans ever. But if the crew you're in makes you feel bad, judged, or invisible? It might be time to mix things up.

Here are a few common dude groups you might run into:

The Sports Bros

- Always sweaty.
- They're constantly tossing a ball.
- Always shouting, "Let's GOOOOOO!" like it's their personal anthem.
- And the uniform? A sports jersey, or you get *the stare*.

The Headphone Heroes

- Hoodie up. Head down.
- Can name five games they play but not five people they've talked to this week.
- They might not say "hi," but will definitely revive you if you die in the video game.
- Not really into eye contact, but solid in a boss fight.

The Style Kings

- Always wearing the latest logo.
- Expensive hoodies. The freshest shoes.
- Judges your outfit before your personality.
- Sometimes nice, sometimes ice.

The Meme Squad

- Lives online even when they're offline.

- Speaks in fluent GIF.
- Tells inside jokes from videos you've never seen.
- Laughs in "LOL's" and speaks in cartoon references.

The Brainy Bunch

- Corrects the teacher (politely... sometimes).
- Competes for the highest grade like it's an Olympic sport.
- Might bring a Rubik's cube to lunch.
- Sometimes secretly stressed about being smart all the time.

The Theater Dudes (Including Band Bros & Artsy Guys)

- Dramatic in *the best way*.
- Randomly starts singing in the middle of lunch.
- Breaks in Shakespeare at the drop of a hat.
- Wears paint-smeared pants or carries drumsticks everywhere.
- Super creative. Super intense. Super ride-or-die.
- Quirky dressers and a black fedora hat.

IMPORTANT:

When I'm talking about these dude groups, there's no judgment here. It's just sort of a fun (and scarily accurate) way to reveal what the groups are and how they act. Throughout my life, I have met all different kinds of guys from all different kinds of groups, and many of them have been pretty amazing, even with **(and often because of)** their unique traits. So make sure *you* don't judge. You could be missing out on someone really great.

But Here's the Thing:

Some of these crews? **Awesome!**

Some of them? **A little judgy.**

Others? **Might even be toxic.**

Sometimes, if you don't walk the walk, talk the talk, or dress exactly like them, you might feel like you're crashing a party you weren't invited to.

And, standing up for yourself doesn't make you dramatic, it makes you smart. **But sometimes, standing up for yourself means just walking away.** Safety first. There's nothing wrong with that. The next time someone's acting like a total tornado, try to remember: Their storm is not your fault. And it's not your job to get soaked.

Just Know:

These are difficult things we're talking about here. Mean people sometimes feel like tigers in the jungle, just waiting for you to show a sign of weakness.

Yeah, this is tough stuff.

But Here's a Big Tip:

You don't need a permission slip to exist. And you definitely don't need to change who you are just to be a part of someone else's group. You don't need a group that makes you *prove yourself.* You need a group that makes you *feel like yourself.*

So What Do You Do?

Great question, young Jedi. Here's your friendship survival kit:

Check the Vibes.

If someone always makes you feel less than great, stressed out, or confused—that's a red flag. Real friends don't make you feel like a sidekick in your own story.

Be *That Guy*.

You know, the one who:

- Includes people who don't have a crew.
- Says "that's not cool" when someone crosses the line (when it's safe to do so).
- Backs up a buddy when someone else picks on him (but remember—safety first. Sometimes walking away with your friend is the right thing to do).
- Doesn't hurt someone just to get laughs.
- Can lose a game without losing their cool.
- Laughs at themselves sometimes. (Because let's be honest, we're all a little goofy.)

Maybe Try to Talk It Out.

- Hard? Yep.
- Scary? A little.
- Powerful? Absolutely.

Saying, "Hey, that hurt," or "Can we talk?" is next level mature. It's how you keep real friendships strong. But don't waste those statements on somebody that's not worthy of your friendship. Those kinds of people are not worth your time.

So, if the table you're sitting at feels more like a test than a friendship? Slide to a new one. Or better yet, build your own group.

And bring snacks.

Because being a good friend? That's real social power.

Final thoughts:

If someone is acting like a mean guy, don't let it wreck your day or your confidence. Their attitude is *not your fault*. Their drama is *not your circus*. And frankly, it says more about them than it does about you.

So yeah, go be awesome! Sit with the kids who make you laugh. Wear your favorite shirt, even if no one else gets it. And if someone is being a jerk? You don't need their permission to walk away.

ACTION TAKEAWAYS:

- Speak up if something feels off (if it's safe to do so).
- Walk away from mean vibes.
- Their bad actions are usually not about you.
- Find or build your own lunch table. Be where you feel comfortable and yourself.
- Be the kind of friend you would want.
- Stay true to yourself.
- If you feel like this is too hard for you to handle on your own, make sure you reach out to your parents or a trusted adult. Sometimes these things are too hard to handle by yourself. And there's nothing wrong with getting help.

12. How Do You Try To Handle Mean Girls, Mean Guys, Bullies, and Cyberbullies?

Bullying… UGHHHHHH. Am I right? Having been a mother and dealing with my kids' school and cyber problems, having been bullied myself, and all the research I have done on the subject, here's what I would tell you first and foremost:

GET HELP EARLY.

That's the biggest takeaway. So, I am going to say it again:

GET HELP EARLY.

Do not wait to get help from your parents or a trusted adult. Don't be embarrassed. It is not a weakness to seek help from others—it is a strength to know that you need a team behind you.

If you feel like you're being bullied, the first plan of attack is to talk to your parents, your coach, or a trusted adult right away. Don't let things boil inside your mind. Don't let these people mess with the magic of your self-esteem and your inner glow. **Just please get help.**

Bullying Is Combination Of...

1. **An imbalance of power:** Their physical size, strength, height, popularity, or if they have embarrassing information about you.
2. **Repetition:** The bad behavior happens over and over.

Bullying also applies to mean girls, mean boys, and cyberbullying. Yes, it is all bullying.

Here's a Game Plan:

When you tell your parents, they will help you assess the situation. Talking it out with them will help a lot. But, the issue may need to include higher authorities.

If you're being bullied at school: You and/or your parents may need to talk to your teacher... then the school counselor... then the school principal... then maybe the school superintendent... and maybe even the State Department of Education... maybe even further.

YES, you are that important.

If you're being bullied online (Cyberbullying): You and your parents need to contact those online site administrators (YouTube, TikTok, Snapchat, Instagram, etc.)

Michelle's Bullying Story:

"When I was about 10 years old, I was bullied. Every day after school, two boys followed me and badgered me as I walked home from school. Every day. I was short and small. They were big and tall. At first, I told them to stop, which unfortunately seemed to excite them. It went on for a long time. Too long. I never told my parents because I was embarrassed. (Big mistake.) I ignored those boys day after day, and finally... finally, it stopped."

If she wouldn't have been a strong person, it could have destroyed her. You can see that she didn't handle it right—she didn't get help from her parents, her coach, or trusted adult. She struggled alone. You need to do better. You need to tell someone. **Take action.**

Where Bullying Happens

Bullying can happen anywhere, but here's where it happens most:

- During school
- After school
- Playgrounds
- On the Bus
- Walking home from School
- Texting
- Online

How to Know If Bullying is Affecting You

Are you acting differently? Feeling nervous? Are you quick to anger? Are you not sleeping well? Have your eating habits changed? Are you staying away from certain situations, like riding the bus or walking home? If so, bullying might be affecting your happiness and it's time to tell someone.

Ideas About How to Handle Bullying

1. Tell Someone: I know we've already talked about this, but it's *that* important. Tell your parents or a trusted adult.

2. Avoid Situations and places where bullying might be.

3. Keep friends around you so that you are never alone on the bus, at your locker, in the hallways, in the bathrooms, or on the way home.

Here are a couple of ideas to try out. Sometimes you'll need to do a little of each or just stick to one that works.

Here's an excellent website: https://StopBullying.gov

This is big stuff we're talking about. Hard stuff. I get it, but it needs to be said.

- **Research it.**
- **Get an adult involved.**
- **Act, don't react.**

Ignore! Ignore! Ignore!:

Ignoring someone's mean behavior is going to be hard, but it's **PROBABLY THE MOST EFFECTIVE WAY TO HANDLE BULLYING** while you're **ALSO** getting help from your parents and trusted adults. It can take a long time to work, but it's worth doing. Ignoring a trash talker by giving them the "cold shoulder" can be a good way to handle bullying or mean behavior without making the situation bigger. By ignoring it, you're taking the energy and power away from them. This means that you:

1. Completely ignore them. You don't want the bully to think they have occupied any part of your thoughts. You want them to think they are unimportant and insignificant—that they don't matter.
2. Never, ever react at all to anything said or done by the mean girls, mean guys, or bullies. Stay calm. Don't let your eyes widen. Don't let your body tense.
3. It's best to even act bored. Just think *"blah blah blah"* when they talk.
4. Don't change your body language at all. Don't startle. Don't let your face fall. Don't slump your shoulders. And whatever you do, don't cry. Continue with the "I'm so bored" routine, but do it with body language. Simply channel your inner

"Ugh, this again?" and maintain that complete *"I'm so over this"* bored attitude.
5. <u>Don't say anything.</u> Nothing. Nada. Zip. Zilch. NOTHING.
6. <u>Just walk away.</u> Casually, not quickly, just walk away.

Kick off the "ignore routine" ASAP and **<u>do it every single time.</u>** Meaning, you can't be wishy-washy about it. You can never react. As soon as the negative behavior begins, you must ignore-ignore-ignore it. Repeat ignoring is very important because if you accidentally react, even one time, you have to start the whole process over from the beginning because then they will then know they *"got to you."* (Uggghhh!) This is a long-term deal. It might take a few days or weeks (or months, DOUBLE UGGGHHH!) for the bully to finally realize that their actions are not affecting you.

<u>**IMPORTANT:**</u> You are combining this "ignore routine" along with talking to an adult about the problem.

Build Your Confidence Armor:

The best defense against mean comments? A strong shield of self-confidence. When you feel good about who you are, mean words just bounce right off you. Work on building your confidence by doing things you enjoy, being proud of what you're good at, and remembering all the awesome feedback you've gotten from people who actually care about you.

The Unfortunate Truth

It's possible that your mean girl/guy/bully has already made up their mind about you. You might not be able to change that vision they have of you. So in that case, really, the only thing you can do in a situation like that is to stay strong, walk away and ignore their destructive behavior and get help from an adult. Just cut them out of your life as much as you can.

A Second Unfortunate Truth

Sadly, people don't always grow out of this. **Sometimes, they just grow up to become OLDER mean girls, mean guys and bullies.** So, now is the best time to try to learn how to deal with people like this.

Talk It Out and Get Help:

And remember—GET AN ADULT INVOLVED. When things get too tough or if things feel unsafe, it's important to recognize that you need help. Please, talk with your parents, your teacher, your school principal, etc., when things get rough. You do not need to handle this alone. They can give you advice on how to handle things and step in if things get to be too much to manage on your own.

Cyberbullies: The Trolls with Wi-Fi

Cyberbullies are like poisonous mosquitoes—they buzz around your phone or computer trying to bite and harm you, but you can totally swat them away.

- **Don't respond:** Trolls love attention, so don't give them the satisfaction. Just ignore, block, and move on.
- Yep—**BLOCK them**. (Yes, I said block.)
- **Save the receipts:** If things get serious, **TAKE SCREENSHOTS** of these conversations, print them out on paper, and show it all to your parents or a trusted adult. Having physical and visual proof helps.
- If it gets too poisonous, delete your account and move on.
- It's important that you see that I said you can **DELETE YOUR ACCOUNT**.

- **Surround yourself with positivity:** Be interested in accounts that make you laugh, smile, or feel inspired. Your feed should feel like a cozy hug, not a war zone.

Do not try to handle cyberbullying on your own. Please **TALK TO SOMEONE,** like your parents, **IMMEDIATELY.** These situations can get very toxic very quickly. Get help and **<u>SHUT IT DOWN</u>.**

Hiding Behind a Mask

A lot of bullies, mean guys and mean girls act the way they do because they're hiding behind their own insecurities. Yep, they're wearing an invisible mask to cover up their own fears, doubts, or struggles. They're hiding behind the mask of the internet. Knowing this doesn't mean you have to excuse their behavior, but it can help you realize one important thing: **It's not about you—it's about them.**

When Someone Lashes Out, Try This:

1. Take a deep breath.
2. Maybe count to 10.
3. Remind yourself, "Their words don't define me."
4. Walk away with your head held high.

Because here's the truth: Your shine is untouchable. Whether someone's hiding behind a mask or trying to drag you into their drama, you've got the power to rise above it. You've got the power now, so grab it, own it, and walk away like the rock star you are.

When Friends Drift to the Dark Side

Imagine one day chilling with your buddy, sharing jokes, planning weekend hangouts, and swapping snacks. Life is good, right? But then—plot twist—your friend starts hanging out with those mean people at school, and suddenly, you're on the outside looking in. Ouch! Let's talk about how to handle this super tricky situation without losing your cool or your confidence.

Understanding the Drift

Understanding why your friend might've teamed up with the mean girls, mean guys or bullies can be really confusing. Sometimes, friends want to fit in so badly that they end up cruising over to the mean crowd, even if they have to be less than nice to others. You'll find yourself standing there scratching your head, thinking, "Who is this person? Where did my friend go?"

Feeling All the Feels

Feeling angry, betrayed, and even super sad about it are all completely valid reactions. Losing a friend this way can be heartbreaking. Give yourself permission to feel all the feelings, but remind yourself you deserve friends who stick by you no matter what crowd they're trying to impress.

Find Your True Crew

Look around. There are loads of other kids who would be happy to hang out with someone as cool as you. It's the perfect time to branch out and make new friends. Join clubs, start a new hobby, or get involved in a sport. Not only will you have fun, but you'll also meet people who love the same things you do.

The Power of Being Positive

Instead of moping about the friend who wandered off to the evil clan, focus on the friends sticking by you. Strengthen those ties. Plan movie nights, go biking, or have a homework party. Positive vibes attract positive people, and that's who you want around you.

Open Door Policy

If your old friend ever decides to come back around, be open to talking things out. People make mistakes, and sometimes they learn from them. Having a heart-to-heart about how their actions hurt, you can clear the air and maybe build a new and better friendship.

Get Support

If you're really feeling down, don't bottle it up. Talk to someone who gets it (maybe a parent, a cool aunt, your coach, or even your school counselor). They can offer advice, comfort, and maybe an idea you hadn't thought of.

Be Drama-Free!

Mean people and bullies don't stand a chance against your kindness, confidence, and classy attitude. Keep lifting others up, dodging the drama traps, and protecting your peace. You're unstoppable, and no one can dim your light!

Building Your Awesome World Beyond School

Okay, so you've noticed the confidence crushers at school are like a storm cloud on a sunny day, right? And it's super easy to feel like school is your whole world. But guess what? There's an entire universe out there filled with wonderful people and great adventures waiting just for you! Let's talk about how to build a fantastic life outside of school that keeps your self-worth shining bright, no matter the school drama.

Discover Your Passions Outside the Classroom

Get into those things you love doing. Maybe you're a secret poet, a future scientist, or an undiscovered sports hero. Join a local club, library group, or sports team that's not connected to the school. These places are gold mines for meeting new friends who share your interests and know nothing about the school's mean-girl and guy or bully drama.

1. Volunteer to Make a Difference: Volunteering is like the superhero version of everyday life. Whether it's helping out at an animal shelter, reading books to younger kids at the library, or helping with food at a local food bank. Giving back makes you feel good about yourself. Plus, you'll meet some awesome people who care about helping others.

2. Find Your Creative Outlet: Creativity isn't only about making art, it's also about expressing who you are. Whether it's writing, drawing, dancing, making videos, or playing an instrument, it's always great to find something that lets you express what's inside. You're in charge when you create, and the mean people can't touch that.

3. Physical Activity for the Win: Getting active isn't just good for your body; it's also great for your mind. When you exercise, your body releases *endorphins* which are the "feel good" chemicals after a workout. So, skate, run, bike, or dance—whatever gets you moving. It's hard to feel down when you're feeling the rush of a good workout!

4. The Buddy System: Even if school feels like a solo mission sometimes, you're not alone. Keep in touch with friends from different schools, a penpal, friends from old neighborhoods, or summer camps. They can be your breath of fresh air when school feels like too much.

5. Family Fun Times: Your family can be a great cheering squad. Plan fun activities with them, like a pizza and movie night, a day trip somewhere new, or help cook dinner together. When you're feeling down, having a strong family bond can remind you that you are valued and appreciated, no matter what.

6. Mind Your Mindfulness: Sometimes, this stuff at school can bog down your brain. Practicing mindfulness or meditation can help clear out the mental junk. There are tons of apps and YouTube channels that can guide you through a relaxing meditation to chill your mind. It's like hitting the reset button for your mood.

7. Journal Your Journey: Keeping a journal isn't just about writing down what happened today, it's also about understanding your feelings, celebrating your wins, and planning your dreams. Then, when you look back, you'll see how much you've grown. And hey, who doesn't like to see their own progress? This is where the ***MY SOCIAL POWER! WORKBOOK*** comes in! It's the right place to journal those thoughts.

You Are Awesome!

Finally, make it a habit to celebrate your wins, no matter how small. Did you get through a tough day? Treat yourself to your favorite snack. Did you finish a tough assignment? One episode of your favorite show is a reward. Celebrating the little things keeps your spirits bright and your focus on what truly matters—YOU!

At the end of the day, the most important thing to remember is that you are amazing just the way you are. Don't let anyone make you doubt that. Your uniqueness is what makes you special. Those who matter—the people who really care about you—will love you for you, no matter what.

There you have it! With all these tips, you'll be more than ready to face any mean moments at school with grace and confidence. Building a life outside of school isn't only about keeping busy; it's about creating a space where you feel good, valued, and excited about the future.

You're way more than your school life, and you've got the whole wide world and more than enough time to prove it! Keep rocking, keep dreaming, and keep being the amazing person you are. Keep your head high, your smile wide, and your heart kind. After all, the world needs more awesome people just like you!

ACTION TAKEAWAYS:

- Mean girls and mean guys are also bullies.
- Mean people often act mean because they are covering up their own insecurities.
- The thrill of the bully's insult is short-lived, so they do it over and over.
- Different ways to deal with bullies: 1. GET HELP FROM YOUR PARENTS or trusted adult. 2. You, with your parents' help, get help from higher authorities. 3. Ignore the bullies and their mean behavior. 4. Build your confidence. 5. Act like they bore you instead of reacting to them. 6. Don't let it get physical. 7. Again, talk it out with someone who can help.
- **These people are telling you who they are, so you should listen.**
- It's possible that you could lose a friend to the mean girl/guy/bully group. Be strong. It's heartbreaking, but it happens.
- Build an awesome world outside of school. Mean people have no power there.
- Look for other ways to enjoy life outside of school: 1. Family Fun. 2. Volunteer. 3. Find a creative outlet. 4. Sports. 5. Mindfulness. 6. Journal.
- Look for opportunities to be a leader.
- The people who really care about you love you no matter what.
- Lastly, again, it's important that you talk to a trusted adult (like your parents, coaches, or principal). I repeat this because *YOU'RE THAT IMPORTANT.*

13. The Peer Pressure Problem

Hey there, trailblazers! Here's something we all bump into: **Peer Pressure.** It's that super awkward feeling when your friends are saying things like, "Come on, everybody's doing it!" It's difficult because sometimes your insides are saying, *"But I kind of don't want to."* It's that conflict of values that causes us to feel pressure.

When we want to be part of the group, but we don't necessarily feel comfortable with what the group is doing—that's peer pressure. But guess what? You're the leader of your own life, and you've got the power to steer your life in any direction you want.

You have the power to say **YES**, and you have the power to say **NO**. Two little words that are actually **GIGANTIC.**

Let's dive into understanding peer pressure, why it's important to stand up to it, and pack our toolbox with strategies to handle it like a pro. If things ever get out of hand, seeking help from your parents, coaches, or a trusted adult is always a smart move.

What Exactly is Peer Pressure?

Imagine you're at lunch, and your buddies are all raving about the latest zombie-themed video game. They nudge you to play, even though you're more into crafting epic LEGO castles. That nudge? That push? That's peer pressure. It's when people try to influence how you act, think, or feel. Sometimes it's bigger, like daring you to prank a teacher. Other times, it's indirect, like feeling the need to wear a certain brand of clothing to fit in or feeling like you need the newest phone or trend to belong.

Peer pressure doesn't only happen in your teenage years. That sneaky force that people use to try to make us do stuff? Yes, unfortunately some people never grow out of it, so learning how to handle it now is a really important skill to have in life. All these skills that you're learning in these chapters and in all my other books <u>are skills that you're going to use for a lifetime</u>!

So, LET'S GET STARTED!

Why Should You Stand Up to Peer Pressure?

Standing up to peer pressure isn't just about saying "no." It's about being true to yourself and making choices that line up with your values and who you are. Here's why it's crucial:

Avoid Trouble: Giving in to negative peer pressure can lead to risky behaviors, like skipping school or trying something unsafe. Standing firm helps you steer clear of unwanted pitfalls.

Build Real Friendships: True friends respect your choices. By standing up to peer pressure, you attract people who appreciate you for who you are.

Staying True to You

So your friends are standing there yelling, "Come on, it'll be fun!" They all have smiles on their faces, laughter in their voices, and they're ready to go, but for some reason there's something in your brain saying, *"This doesn't feel like something I should be doing."* But, you're also standing there thinking that you're going to be missing out on some kind of fun experiences if you don't go along with the crowd.

Yeah, I get it, and it's hard.

But...

- What if it feels like what they're saying really sounds like no big deal? Maybe *this time* it's not a big deal. But what if it turns out that it *is* a big deal? Are you feeling good that you said "Yes" just to fit in?
- Maybe that thing they want you to do is slightly dangerous? Outside your comfort zone? What about then? Are you saying "Yes" then?
- Maybe they're telling you one thing, but secretly they have a plan to do something completely different that goes against your rules... your religion... your values... your safety? What about then? Are you feeling good about saying "Yes" then?
- Maybe they're asking you to do this one small thing *this* time to get you in the *habit* of saying "Yes." This is called *grooming*. They're leaning into you yelling, "Yeah! You're

our *YES MACHINE!* Come on, let's go!" Then later they pressure you to do things more questionable each time you go with them because you always say "Yes." Does that sound like a good situation to be in?
- Are you a *"YES MACHINE?"* Are you still feeling good about blindly saying "Yes" to people that are pressuring you? Are you becoming someone who always says *YES?*

YIKES! Those are some heavy-duty questions I just threw at you. Let's bring it down a notch! Just know, I'm not judging you. I'm just wanting you to see things for the way they are. You don't want to get caught up in something that isn't YOU.

There's a reason why you're feeling that pressure, and **it's normally because something about it feels *wrong*.** That feeling of wrongness? That's your intuition talking, your *spidey-sense*. And when your intuition is talking, you should probably listen.

My point here is that sometimes what people *say* can be completely different from what they actually *do,* and you don't want to get caught up in a tidal wave of peer-pressured bad decisions.

You Have the Power to Stand Tall and Be Your Own Awesome Self!

It might seem easier to just do what your *friends* are asking you to do, but following the crowd might lead you away from what you genuinely enjoy or believe in. Embracing your uniqueness is what makes you stand out in the best possible way.

The Bright Side: Positive Peer Pressure

Not all peer pressure is bad! Sometimes friends can inspire you to try new activities, study harder, or pick up healthy habits. Surround yourself with peers and friends who lift you up and encourage you to be your best self.

Tools in Your Toolbox: Strategies to Handle Peer Pressure

Equip yourself with these handy tools to navigate peer pressure with confidence:

1. The Power of No: The "Nah, I'm good" Move

Imagine this: A group of people try to get you to go to a party where there's going to be alcohol, but you feel like alcohol is not your thing, and you'd rather spend your time with your new pet goldfish. When they bug you to come to the party, flash a smile and say, "Nah, my pet goldfish and I have a championship-level splash routine to rehearse." —Boom!—you've just dodged peer pressure with style and a little bit of humor!

2. The Buddy System

Ever notice how superheroes often have sidekicks? Batman has Robin, and you can have your own trusty sidekick too. Find a friend who shares your values; someone who can back you up when peer pressure strikes. Together, you're an unstoppable duo against any unwanted pressure.

3. The "Change the Channel" Trick

Let's say your friends are talking trash about the new kid, but you're not into spreading rumors. Channel your inner TV remote and change the subject: "Speaking of new, did you see the latest episode of that cool science show?" Suddenly, the conversation shifts, and you've steered clear of all that negativity.

4. The Exit Strategy

Picture this: You're at a party, and someone suggests playing a prank on the grumpy neighbor. Not your idea of fun? Time to activate your exit strategy. Maybe you suddenly remember you promised your cat a dance-off, or that your "pet rock" is expecting a movie night. Whatever the excuse, make your graceful exit and avoid getting roped into trouble.

5. The "Superhero Pose" Confidence Boost

Did you know that standing like a superhero can actually make you feel more confident? The next time you're facing peer pressure, strike a power pose—chin slightly raised, shoulders back, hands on hips, feet apart—and take a deep breath. You'll feel ready to take on the world, or at least say "no" with confidence.

6. The "Blame It On the Grown-Ups" Card

When all else fails, don't hesitate to use the classic: "My parents would ground me for a century if I did that." It's amazing how the threat of eternal grounding can get you out of sticky situations. It's a great way to keep the peace without offending anyone.

When to Get an Adult Involved

Sometimes peer pressure can spiral beyond our control. **If you ever feel threatened, unsafe, or unsure, it's important to bring in an adult.** They can provide guidance, support, and get involved, if necessary. Asking for help is a shows strength, not weakness.

Being true to yourself is way cooler than following the crowd. So, the next time peer pressure comes knocking, use these tricks to stand your ground and keep being the amazing, unique person you are. You've got this!

Quiz Time! How Would You Handle These Situations?

1. The Sneaky Snack Swipe: You're at a friend's house, and their mother just baked fresh chocolate chip cookies. They suggest taking cookies from the kitchen without asking. What do you do?

- A. Join in, it's just a cookie.
- B. Politely decline and suggest asking for permission first.
- C. Take the cookie, but feel guilty later.
- D. Make an excuse and leave the room.

2. The Daring Dare: During a break time at school, a group dares you to climb the tallest tree, even though it's against school rules. How do you respond?

- A. Climb the tree to impress them.
- B. Laugh it off and suggest a safer game.
- C. Tell them you're afraid and walk away.
- D. Agree, but secretly plan to back out.

3. The Exclusion Exploration: Your friends decide to exclude a classmate from your group project because they think they're "weird." What do you do?

- A. Go along with the group to avoid conflict.
- B. Stand up for the classmate and include them in the project.

C. Stay silent and let the group decide.
D. Talk to the classmate privately, but not involve them in the project.

4. The Fashion Frenzy: Everyone in your group is wearing a new, expensive brand of shoes, and they tease you for not having it. What do you do?

A. Beg your parents to buy it for you.
B. Confidently wear what you've got and ignore the teasing.
C. Avoid your friends until you can get the new gear.
D. Pretend you don't care, but feel embarrassed inside.

Best Answers and Explanations

1. **B) Politely decline and suggest asking for permission first.** Respecting others' property is essential. Suggesting to ask for permission shows integrity and sets a positive example.
2. **B) Laugh it off and suggest a safer game.** Deflecting peer pressure with humor and proposing something different keeps things fun without breaking rules or risking safety.
3. **B) Stand up for the classmate and include them in the project.** Inclusivity and kindness are vital. Standing up for others fosters a supportive community.
4. **B) Confidently wear your current shoes and ignore the teasing.** Choosing to wear your current sneakers with confidence demonstrates assurance and strength against peer pressure.

Peer Presssure Cheat Codes

- ✔ Listen to your gut.
- ✔ You don't owe anyone a "yes."
- ✔ It's OK to walk away.
- ✔ Find your voice and find your people
- ✔ You're worth isn't up for debate.

There you have it, my friends! Don't bow down to peer pressure. Only do things that line up with who you are.

Now get out there and do great things!

ACTION TAKEAWAYS:

- Peer pressure is when friends or people around you try to influence your choices—good or bad—by making you feel like you have to "fit in."
- The activity that they're asking you to join in might be something small or it might be something big.
- Pressure is created when the act of saying yes or joining in actually feels like it conflicts with your inner values or feels *wrong*.
- It's important to stay true to your beliefs, even when people are pressuring you to do what they want you to do.
- Saying NO to peer pressure can be hard.
- Sometimes saying yes to peer pressure can put you in a dangerous position.
- You have the power to stand tall and be your awesome self.
- Utilize the six tools in your peer pressure toolbox to help you say NO to things that don't line up with who you are. They are: 1. The Power of No: The "Nah, I'm good" Move, 2. The Buddy System, 3. The "Change the Channel" Trick, 4. The Exit Strategy, 5. The "Superhero Pose" Confidence Boost, 6. The "Blame It On the Grown-Ups" Card.

- Always reach out to an adult if things get out of hand. If you're feeling too much pressure and need to bounce ideas off someone else, your parents or a trusted adult are a great place to start.

14. Social Media Safety: We're Getting Real!

Social media is super fun for staying connected with friends and sharing cool stuff. But let's help you figure out how to keep it positive on social media, keep it safe, and understand how it can affect how you see yourself. Let's teach you how to be smart about what you're looking at and doing online.

- **Don't Let It Measure Your Worth:** It's easy to only think about counting likes or studying comments. But your value isn't about the number of likes you get; you're worth way more than that.
- **Mean Comments:** Sometimes, people can be harsh or rude on the internet. That negativity can really hurt your feelings and mess with how you see yourself. Don't let that happen to you. Limit your friends, and know that it's okay to **block** harsh or toxic people.

How to Keep Things Fun and Healthy

Choose who you *follow* wisely. Create a happier online space by *following* friends and accounts that make you feel good, not ones that cause you to doubt yourself.

- **Real Friends:** Make your online circle exactly like your real-life one—you know, your buds from school or in sports. Fill it with friends you really know. Stick with people who genuinely care about you and ditch the online drama.
- **Set Time Limits:** Don't let social media eat up all your time. Too much scrolling can make you miss out on the real fun. It can also bring you down if you're not careful.

Okay, digital explorers! This is the wild world of the internet, where not everything is as it seems. It's kind of like a magician's hat. It's full of surprises, but not all of them are cute bunnies.

All That Glitters Is Not Gold. Sometimes It's Just Glitter

Jumping online is like diving into a treasure chest, but not everything that glitters is gold. Sometimes, it's just shiny junk. Because something looks awesome or everyone else is talking about it doesn't mean it's the real deal. It's like those photos of mega-amazing cheeseburgers you see in the ads. Have you ever noticed they never look that yummy in real life? Yep, the internet can also be like that—super cheesy, but not always in a yummy way.

So, when you "*follow*" someone, make sure they're a good person to follow.

IMPORTANT INSIGHT:

Personally, I sort of have a problem with the modern usage of the word "*follower*" in social media. It supports that mean kid/bully social structure that makes it seem like some people are better or more important than you (FALSE!). It's just that right now, at this moment, those people you're considering on social media might just be more popular than you, more famous, or have an interesting skill.

HOWEVER, someday YOU also might have all of those cool attributes, including an interesting skill that you just haven't discovered yet. AND, you could become famous for something, we just don't know yet! Your life has only just begun!

Seeing the word "*follower*" everywhere makes the word so common in your vocabulary that **you might think that your role in life is to follow everybody. When, in fact, your important role in life could be to <u>LEAD!</u>** So, NO! *Following* is not your role.

Let's make a campaign to live in the world of being a "Leader" more often instead of being a *follower*.

When you click the "*follow*" button on a site, I would love for you to have this mental note instead: I want you to think "I'm *Interested*" *instead* of thinking "I'm *following*." Let's be *interested* in something or someone instead of just *following*. Being interested is active participation, while *following* is just being a passive sponge.

I know, you're probably thinking, "*Follower.* It's only a *word...*" Yeah, you're right, but **words matter.** How do you feel when someone compliments you? Great, right? Well, those are just words... And when someone insults you? Pretty crummy, right? All of those are just words... But all of those words have power over you. Do you see where I'm going here? **WORDS MATTER.**

My Dad Used to Always Say: "Everyone's Entitled to Their Own Stupid Opinion"

Mean comments are flying around online like popcorn at a movie theater. Not all opinions matter. Some comments are just plain stupid, and some are just plain mean. You don't have to listen to all that negative *noise*.

So, if someone is being rude, here's what you do: Scroll on by! Don't even think twice about it, okay? Think of it as steering your spaceship away from the dark side of the moon.

Be the Boss of Your Online World!

It's super important to hang out on sites where you can control who is peeking into your digital diary.

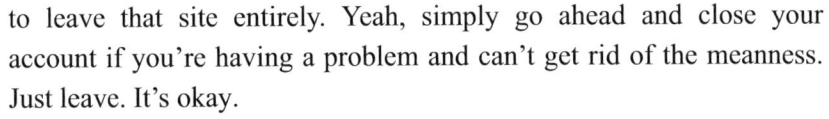

If you can't control who sees what you post or who's sending you messages, it might be time to leave that site entirely. Yeah, simply go ahead and close your account if you're having a problem and can't get rid of the meanness. Just leave. It's okay.

Being able to pick your online pals makes you the captain of your own ship, cruising the high seas of the internet with your own chosen crew.

NEW MANTRA:

"If I Can't Control It, Do I Really Want to Scroll It?"

It's okay if sometimes a site isn't the right fit for you. It's like wearing something that doesn't fit right—uncomfortable and not your vibe. If you find yourself on a site where you can't control who sees your info, it's like leaving your diary open in the school lunchroom. Would you really want to do that? Of course

Social Media Safety: We're Getting Real!

not! So maybe, just maybe, it's time to say "bye-bye!" and find a new digital playground.

The internet can feel like everyone is wearing masks. It's totally okay to show the real you, but you don't need to tell the world *everything.* Let me say that again:

You Don't Need to Tell the World Everything. You really don't.

Yeah, it might be cool to share a photo of that awesome dessert or your new favorite drink, but you don't need to tell the world everything about your inside story.

Social Media Safety: Fasten Your Seat Belts

While we're at it, let's get into some pretty important stuff here.

It's important to know that even though it might seem like it, **your online life is NOT your REAL LIFE.**

SMART SAFETY RULES

IMPORTANT! Here Are Some Don'ts

Here are some DON'Ts regarding anyone you meet online or in a chat room. Sorry, but this needs to be said. If you don't already know these people in your REAL LIFE:

1. DON'T give them your telephone number.
2. DON'T give them your address.
3. DON'T give them your current location.
4. DON'T give them your school name.
5. DON'T give them your friends' names or location information.
6. DON'T give any sensitive information, like bank account numbers or any of your parents' information—NOTHING.

7. <u>DON'T</u> get into a car with someone you met online or anyone that you and your parents don't know AND TRUST in real life.
8. <u>DON'T</u> meet someone somewhere that you met online, <u>day or night</u>. <u>JUST DON'T</u>.
9. <u>DON'T</u> accept friend requests from strangers. Be careful about accepting friend requests or messages from people you don't know in real life.
10. <u>DON'T</u> over-share on social media. Sharing too much on social media, like your routines, vacations, or personal life, can be harmful because this can be used to track you or impersonate you.
11. <u>DON'T</u> post sensitive content. Avoid posting anything online that you wouldn't want everyone (including strangers) to see. This includes personal photos, location tags, and future plans.
12. <u>DON'T</u> post when you're angry or upset. Avoid posting or responding online when your emotions are in high drive. This can lead to regrettable decisions. Sleep on it. Let yourself cool down.
13. <u>DON'T</u>, even if you've been chatting with them for days, weeks, months or years, <u>DON'T</u> do any of the above. It might seem like after all that time that you "know" them. <u>YOU DON'T</u>. Bad people often pretend and say things you want to hear just to get access to you.
14. All of these <u>DON'T</u>s apply whether it's <u>DAY OR NIGHT</u>.
15. <u>AND TALK TO YOUR PARENTS!</u> Don't be shy about your safety. Talk with your parents and get them involved in what you're doing. They're on your side and they want you to succeed in life and also be safe.

DON'T DO ANYTHING TO JEOPARDIZE YOUR SAFETY!

There are more safety rules, but these are only the *biggies*.

Uuuuughhhh!!! Okay, I know what I just said was totally creepy, and to be honest, it freaks me out, too.

<u>BUT, IT'S REAL</u>. Even adults get lured into some of these things, things that can be dangerous.

Sorry, but it had to be said.

Okay—Whew!—new subject!!!

Taking a Break From Social Media

Now and then, take a break from screens and apps. Try taking a social media vacation for a week. Sounds crazy? I know! It seems almost impossible to ask, but when we get all of that digital clutter out of our mind, it actually makes things really peaceful.

Social Media Vacation Ideas

- Try a craft challenge.
- Redecorate your room.
- Bake something wild and weird.
- Make your own mood board.
- Create a "Future Me" Vision poster.
- Invent a new dance routine (maybe with a friend!)
- Write a note to a friend (Yes, on paper!)
- Interview your grandparents or older relatives about their life.
- Journal in your ***MY SOCIAL POWER! WORKBOOK!***

The list is endless!

So, get out there and build your real-world confidence. Spend more time *doing* stuff that makes you feel awesome offline, like sports, art, or just hanging out. Real-life fun builds real confidence and connection.

Be Smart, Be Safe, and Keep It Real!

Traveling through the internet is like being a superhero in your own comic book. You have all the power to choose your path, dodge the trolls under the bridge, and shine like the star you are!

Always be smart, stay safe, and remember, **the best version of you is the <u>real you</u>.**

Go ahead, power up your screens, and make the digital world a little brighter with your awesomeness. Keep it real. Keep it safe. Keep it rocking in your own amazing way! **And if someone gets mean, kick them to the curb.**

ACTION TAKEAWAYS:

- Limit online friends to real friends. Don't tolerate mean comments. It's okay to block people or leave a site.
- Set time limits online. Take a social media vacation.
- Try to change your way of thinking to "I'm Interested" instead of "I'm a *Follower*."
- Words matter.
- Look for opportunities to be a leader.
- <u>IMPORTANT: Read and keep safe by doing all 15 of the SMART SAFETY RULES.</u>
- It's important to incorporate your parents in your online safety.

Here Are Some More Online Safety Tips:

16. <u>DON'T</u> use weak passwords. Don't use easily guessable passwords like "password123". And try to avoid reusing passwords on other sites.

Social Media Safety: We're Getting Real!

17. <u>DON'T</u> share your passwords.
18. <u>DON'T</u> click on suspicious links. Don't click on links in emails, texts, or pop-ups from people you don't know. These could be harmful and contain viruses or malware.
19. <u>DON'T</u> ignore your privacy settings. They're there to protect your info.
20. <u>DON'T</u> forget to log out when you leave the site, especially on shared computers.
21. <u>DON'T</u> forget to have your parents update your operating system, apps, and antivirus software regularly.
22. <u>DON'T</u> download any unverified software or apps. Ask for your parents' help.
23. <u>DON'T</u> forget to use two-factor authentication (2FA). Don't skip securing your computer and your accounts with two-factor authentication for an extra layer of security.
24. <u>DON'T</u> overlook the signs of a scam. Be aware of common scam tactics and don't ignore red flags like offers that seem too good to be true. Please involve your parents in this.
25. <u>DON'T</u> use public Wi-Fi for sensitive transactions. Avoid conducting online banking or shopping over an unsecured public Wi-Fi network.
26. <u>DON'T</u> try to bypass firewalls and antivirus protection. Keep these protections active to keep your devices safe from online threats.
27. And please, **<u>involve your parents</u>**.

15. The Friendship Shift: Why is Everyone Acting So Weird?

One second, your friends are all about getting together, snacks, and riding bikes around the neighborhood like you own the place. The next? People are suddenly forming cliques, whispering about crushes, and talking about stuff like "social status," whatever that means. It's like someone flipped a switch, and you're standing there thinking, "Wait, did I miss the memo?"

Real Talk: When Friendships Start Feeling... Weird

Meet Leila. Leila had her best friends, and everything was awesome. They've been tight since second grade, and their group had inside jokes and fun giggles. But then, something started changing. Suddenly, everyone was acting... different.

One of her besties, Harper, started hanging out with a new crew. She turned into someone who suddenly cared a lot about appearances, popularity, and scrolling her phone 24/7. Like, a lot. Instead of cracking jokes and playing their favorite games, Harper was always glued to her phone and talking about people Leila didn't even know.

And the weirdest part? When Leila tried to talk about their usual fun stuff, Harper would just roll her eyes and say, "OMG, that's so childish." (Excuse me? Who decided that fun has an expiration date?!)

At first, Leila felt like she had to change, too. Like maybe if she acted cooler or pretended to care about whatever was so fascinating about Harper's new crowd, she wouldn't feel left out.

But here's the thing about pretending to be someone you're not—it gets exhausting. Big time.

What if I'm the *Harper*?

Do you feel like you're the friend that is *changing?* Do you feel like you're drifting to a new friendship? People grow and change, and that's OK! Just don't forget about the people who've always had your back. Change as part of life, but respect is always cool.

The Awkward Reality of Social Friendship Shifts

It's totally normal for friendships to change as people grow. It's also totally normal to feel weird when it happens.

It's kind of like when you and your best friends used to love peanut butter and jelly sandwiches. But now? Some of them are all about sushi, and suddenly PB&J is "stupid." It's not that PB&J stopped being awesome, it's just that *their* tastes changed.

Friendships can be the same way.

The Friendship Shift: Why is Everyone Acting So Weird?

But guess what? That doesn't mean you have to ditch what you used to love just to fit in.

Leila's Social Power Move

One day, Leila figured out that if she had to work this hard to keep a friendship going, then maybe it wasn't the right fit anymore.

So, instead of chasing after Harper's approval, she did something totally unexpected…

She went back to being herself.

She started hanging out with other kids who still thought climbing trees was cool, who still loved to laugh until they couldn't laugh anymore, and who definitely didn't make her feel like she needed to change to be accepted.

And guess what? Leila was so much happier.

The best part? A few months later, Harper actually started coming back around. Turns out, being "cool" all the time? Exhausting. And Leila? She never stopped being fun.

So… What Do You Do When This Happens to You?

If you're feeling like friendships are getting weird, here's your social power move:

- **Don't force it.** If a friendship is shifting, let it. If you have to change who you are to keep it, then it's not worth it.
- **Find your people.** The best friends are the ones who like you for you, not because you're trying to keep up with them.
- **It's OK to miss what used to be.** Because things have to

change doesn't mean you can't look back on the fun times you both had together and appreciate them.
- **New friendships are waiting for you.** Sometimes, when old friendships fade, new (and even better) ones can take their place.

Your Social Power Move

Leila didn't change who she was to keep a friendship alive. She let things shift naturally, and focused on what made her happy; she wound up with a stronger group of friends. You can do that, too!

So, if you ever feel like friendships are changing around you, remember this: **The right people will always make space for you.**

Now, go find your crew. Friendship shifts happen. But always remember to maintain the magic of YOU. You've got this!

ACTION TAKEAWAYS:

- Sometimes friendships change, and that's okay.
- Trying to *fit* into social situations can be exhausting.
- You don't have to stop doing the things you love just to fit in with a certain group. Maybe that group is not for you.
- Don't force friendships. Just be YOU.
- Best friends like you for who you are.
- You can still look back on fun times you had with old friends.
- New friendships are waiting for you. People who are your kind of people will always have space for you in their life.

16. Chill Out and Find Your Zen

Ugghh, stress, I know, right? Stress is like carrying a super heavy backpack around all day—it weighs you down. When you're stressed out about your social confidence or how you look, it makes the "backpack" feel even heavier.

Literally, a zillion things can create stress: Pressures at school, changes in friendships, problems at home, moving, handling chores, too many activities, the list goes on.

With all these crazy things going on in Stress Town, it's important to know that you're not the only person with all these pressures. Everybody feels stress. Let's find out how to spot when you're stressed. Understanding how it also might be linked to how you see your body and your social life is a cool way to lighten that load.

Spotting Signs of Stress

Mood swings

If you feel irritable out of nowhere, it might be stress messing with you. When you've got a ton of homework, a big game coming up, or drama with friends, it's like your emotions are on a wild rollercoaster—up one minute and down the next.

Stress messes with your brain, making you feel all sorts of moodiness. One second you're chill, and the next you're thinking, "Why is everyone so annoying?!" This is a typical reaction to all the things we juggle every day.

Not Sleeping?

If you're lying in bed thinking about a million things, tossing and turning all night and just can't hit the snooze button (Gaaaah!)—t's so frustrating! It's often because stress is hanging out with you.

Yeah, it's probably stress doing its thing. You're stressing over a test or freaking out about a fight with your best friend. Your brain gets all buzzy and won't chill out. This makes it super hard to catch those Zzz's. Basically, your mind keeps racing about all the stuff you've got to do or what went wrong today—and BOOM!—there goes your sleep. It's like your brain refuses to take a break even when you're super tired. Ugh, so annoying.

Feeling Tired All the Time?

And what about those times when you actually do sleep, and you still feel wiped out when you wake up? Or when you feel like you're tired all the time, even if you didn't do much? Well, guess what? That's stress again.

Chill Out and Find Your Zen

When you're stressed, even over small stuff, your body acts like it's working overtime. It's like your energy gets zapped even though you're not doing much of anything. You feel exhausted for no reason. Yes, stress might be the sneaky villain.

Signs of Stress

Negative Thoughts

You know when you've got those negative thoughts that just won't quit? Like your brain is on repeat with stuff like, "I can't do this!" or "What if I mess up?" Yup, you guessed it—stress.

Stress can make your thoughts feel crummy and make everything seem worse than it actually is. It's like watching a movie that's all doom and gloom, and you can't find the remote to change the channel. Stress kind of cranks up the volume on all those bad vibes, making it super hard to see the nicer side of life.

If you find your brain is going down those dark thought tunnels, it's probably stress pulling the strings. It can make you see things in a not-so-great light, including how you look and feel about yourself and your life. You might start worrying more about your body or feeling bad about yourself. Yeah, it stinks.

Avoiding Stuff

Ever start ditching swim parties or not wanting to do things because you're not feeling great about how you look or how you feel? Do you ever find yourself totally dodging stuff that you've got to do, like homework, cleaning your room, or even texting back your friends? That might be stress playing hide-and-seek with you.

When you're stressed, sometimes your brain says, "Nope, not today" and you end up putting off even simple things. It's kind of like your mind puts up a giant "Out of Order" sign.

The problem is that when you avoid stuff, it adds up and makes it feel even bigger. It's like a giant mountain of *"I can't even tackle this now. It's too big."* Yeah, it's a tough cycle to be in.

PERSONAL SIDE STORY:

Okay, so there was one day where everything just felt *off*. I woke up late. I couldn't find my favorite jacket, and to top it off, I had a pop quiz in math. By lunchtime, I was a stress ball ready to explode.

But then, I remembered something my friend told me: *"When things get crazy, just hit the pause button."* So, I took a deep breath—like, a really deep one right there in the middle of lunch. I probably looked a little weird, but I didn't care. I just needed a minute to chill.

After that, I went to the gym locker room and got my running shoes. Running always had a way of calming me down; like it just pumped it out of me. When I finished, a lot of that stress load was gone.

By the time my friends found me, I was feeling a lot better.

Then, I decided to talk it out with my best friend, Jordan. I talked about my rough morning, and my friend nodded and said, "Yeah, I totally get it. Puberty is whack." We both looked at each other and started laughing. Knowing that I wasn't alone somehow made everything seem less intense.

Finally, I reminded myself that it's okay to mess up sometimes. Looking back, those times when I messed up seem like the times I learned the most. I didn't ace that math quiz, but hey, it wasn't the end of the world. I told myself, "You've got this. One bad day doesn't define you."

So yeah, stress happens in your social life, especially with all the changes going on in your life right now. But now I know that when it hits, I can pause, breathe, do something I enjoy, and talk to someone I trust. It doesn't make the stress disappear, but it makes it a whole lot easier to handle. And honestly? That's pretty cool.

How to Manage Stress Like a Boss!

Mindfulness

Here's a cool trick to kick stress to the curb: Mindfulness! Mindfulness is all about living in the moment and not stressing about yesterday or what's going on in the future. **The trick is that you only think about RIGHT NOW.** It helps you chill out and be less freaked by all the stuff going on.

Mindfulness is paying super close attention to what's happening right now, like how you're breathing or what sounds you hear. It's about being right where you are (right now in this moment) instead of worrying about tomorrow's math test or that awkward text conversation you had with a bunch of friends.

Practicing mindfulness is like saying *"Wait a second!"* in the crazy video game of life. It helps clear up all the noise in your head and makes things feel a bit easier. It's a great way to give your brain a mini vacation from Stress Town.

Relaxation Techniques

Another awesome way to deal with stress is to try some relaxation techniques. Think of them like cheat codes for when you're feeling super wound up.

Do Stuff Like:

- **Try a Little Distraction:** Do what relaxes you. Maybe listen to music, draw, or watch funny videos. Sometimes, concentrating on puzzles, playing a video game, or a game with your family really takes your mind off what is bothering you.
- **Breathing Exercises:** Take a slow breath in, hold it for a few seconds, and let it out even slower. Do this a few times and feel the stress simply float away.
- **Guided Imagery:** Close your eyes and picture yourself in a super calm place, like a beach or a quiet forest.
- **Exercise:** Exercise is a wonderful stress buster. When you work your body and focus on your exercise skills, you tend to forget about the stress. Yoga, soccer, running, you name it, exercise is powerful! It works out all those tense muscles and feels really great!

These tricks can help your mind and body hit the reset button. They make you feel way more Zen and ready to tackle whatever comes your way.

Get Organized

Sometimes stress comes from feeling like you've got too much going on. Keeping a planner or setting up a to-do list can help you feel in control and less overwhelmed by your schedule. When you cross things off your list, you feel a sense of accomplishment. It lightens the load and lessens the stress. Why don't you try the *MY SOCIAL POWER! WORKBOOK*?!

Getting yourself organized will totally get rid of a lot of stress. When your room, backpack, or desk is a giant mess, it's like your brain gets cluttered, too. So, sort out your school papers, line up your shoes, or even color-code your history notes. It's like putting together a puzzle; everything fits into the right spot, and you wind up feeling super satisfied.

When everything is neat and where it should be, you spend less time looking for stuff and more time relaxing. Trust me, once you get organized, your whole day flows smoother, and you feel way less stressed.

Talk About It

Talking it out with someone is like when the garbage truck comes by your neighborhood and takes all your trash away. Talking about all the things bothering you is the same way, it takes away the stress garbage. When stuff is bugging you, chatting with a friend, a parent, or even a teacher can make a huge difference. They help you carry that load. Talking is like letting air out of a super puffed-up balloon. Whew, you can finally relax. Your special someone's help can calm you down, help you gain a new perspective, or simply provide a listening ear.

Saying things out loud makes them seem way less scary than they do in your head. When they buzz around in your head, they feel bigger and bigger.

Next time you get all tangled up inside with stress, just talk it out. It seriously helps to share what's going on. It's like hitting the refresh button on your mood. Talking about how you feel can lighten your load a lot. You don't have to handle everything on your own. Your mind and body will thank you.

Having a Support Crew

When you're feeling all twisted up inside because of stress, your support crew can seriously help flip the script on how you feel. Someone could jump in with an idea you never thought of. Then suddenly, everything seems brighter!

Having a solid group of friends, family, or even teachers means you've got people who can throw you a new perspective or remind you that you're not alone in this. They can help you see things in a fresh way, making problems seem a lot smaller.

Knowing you have a great support system ready to back you up at any moment can make all the difference when the stress monster shows up.

Next time you're stressed, reach out and watch the magic happen as they help you see the brighter side of things. Knowing you've got people who care about you can make all the difference. Knowing that you're not alone is huge. They can cheer you on, help you laugh, and listen when you need to let it all out.

The Signs of "Ugh" Stress

Stress is like that annoying mosquito buzzing around in your head—it's hard to ignore, and it makes everything feel worse. Sometimes, stress is helpful (like when it reminds you to study for that big test), but most of the time, it just feels like, "Ugh." But, the good news? You can learn to swat that stress away and grow a mindset that makes you feel like a total boss, no matter what life throws at you.

Tips for Growing a Resilient Mindset

Building a resilient mindset is like training your brain to handle stress better. It's kind of like working out, but with way fewer squats. Here's how to start:

Chill Out and Find Your Zen

- **Breathe like a pro:** When stress starts creeping in, stop and take five deep breaths. Breathe in through your nose, and gently blow it slowing out your mouth. Pretend you're blowing out birthday candles on the world's biggest cake.
- **Flip the script:** Instead of saying, "I can't handle this," try "This is tough, but I've got this." Turning a negative thought into a positive one and turning off your inner critic is like giving your brain a pep talk.
- **Shrink the problem:** Ask yourself, "Will this matter in a week? A month? A year?" Most of the time, the answer is nope! Suddenly, it doesn't feel so big anymore.
- **Move your body:** Dance, jump, stretch, or even walk your dog (or imaginary dog—it works! Hahaha!). Physical movement tells your brain, "We're shaking off the stress, baby!"
- **Talk it out:** Stress loves to grow when you keep it bottled up. Tell a trusted friend, family member, or even your pet hamster what's bugging you. Sharing = Caring (for your mind.)
- **Celebrate your wins:** Got through a tough day? High-five yourself. Finished a project? Do a little happy dance. Recognizing how strong you are builds your resilience muscle.

Stress doesn't have to win, superstar. With these tips, you'll be turning "Ugh stress" into "I've got this!" in no time. You're stronger than you think, and every time you tackle a tough moment, you're strengthening your resilience muscle and your proving that you're strong. Go YOU!

Today is Only One Day, Tomorrow Will Be Better!

Hey, even if today totally stunk, guess what? Tomorrow is a brand new day full of new opportunities!

If things didn't go your way today, maybe you bombed a quiz, or had a fall-out with a friend. Don't sweat it! Tomorrow is a fresh start where anything can happen. It's all about keeping that hope alive.

Knowing that tomorrow is there is like knowing you have a reset button in the game of life. Super powerful!

Try to think about the cool stuff that can happen next in your life, like acing that test you studied for, or making up with your buddy, or getting the lead in the play you auditioned for, or even someday inventing the cure for cancer! Hey, it could happen!

So, toss today's stress in the trash and get pumped for a better tomorrow. Every new day is a chance to make something awesome happen!

ACTION TAKEAWAYS:

- Monitor your signs of stress: Mood swings, tiredness, negativity, avoiding things.
- Practice mindfulness: Live in the moment, the right now.
- Take a moment to relax. Find your Zen.
- Exercise is always good for stress.
- Organizing your space helps organize your mind. Try the ***MY SOCIAL POWER! WORKBOOK*** for this!
- Talk it out. Let someone help carry the load.
- Tomorrow will be better. Tomorrow is another day!

17. Find Your People, Find Your Power!

Ever feel like you're stuck on an island of awkwardness, just waving a tiny flag that says, "Someone talk to me!"? Yeah, we've all been there. But guess what? You're not actually alone. The world is filled with people. And some of them? They are totally *your* people!

The trick is finding your own support squad—your group of awesome humans who hype you up, have your back, and make your life so much easier. Having a strong social circle isn't only about not sitting alone at lunch (though, let's be honest, that's a bonus). It's about having people who help you grow, cheer you on, and make life a lot more fun.

So, let's talk about building your ultimate social squad; the dream team that makes you feel strong, confident, and ready to take on the world!

Strengths and Weaknesses: Everyone's Got Them

Nobody is flawless. Not even that kid in your class who somehow has perfect hair every single day. We all have strengths (pluses +'s) and weaknesses (minuses -'s). Part of building a solid social squad is finding people who balance you out.

Maybe you're great at giving pep talks, but feel terrible at math—Boom! It comes to you!—You need a buddy who can explain fractions without making your brain melt. Maybe you're an idea machine, but you need someone who can actually turn those ideas into action—Boom again!—these people that you need can be part of your support crew!

And the best squads? They're full of people who are like puzzle pieces that fit together perfectly; everyone bringing something different, and together you make something amazing!

Why Having a Support Crew is Everything

Imagine if *The Avengers* had just one hero. Like Iron Man, but all by himself? *Meh.* It's the whole team that makes them unstoppable. That's how your friend group should be: A social power squad where each person brings their own special skills to the mix.

Here's the deal:

- **You learn from each other:** Your friend walks in like they own the place? Take some notes.
- **You grow together:** They push you to try new things, like karaoke, or talking to your crush. (Gasp!)
- **You support each other:** Bad day? Your support crew lifts you up. Or a big win? They're there cheering the loudest.

A great social support crew is like a cheat code for life—it makes everything a little easier, a lot more fun, and much less scary.

Real Talk: "What Do You Bring to the Table?"

In companies all over the world, people often gather around conference tables for business meetings. Each person brings something different and important to the table for the group's goal.

1. One person might be super creative: meaning they know how to *"create"* the goal.
2. One person might be great at strategy: meaning they know how to *"accomplish"* the goal.
3. One person might be great at marketing: meaning they know how to *"sell"* the goal.
4. One person might be great at art: meaning they know how to *"visually demonstrate"* the goal.
5. One person might be good at safety: meaning they know how to *"safely build"* the goal.
6. One person might be great with money: meaning they know how to *"pay"* for the goal.

Do you see where I'm going here? Everybody *"brings something to the table."* The same thing happens in your support crew: Everybody in your group "brings something to the table"—you included!

It's not only about what you *get* from your social group, it's also about what you *bring* to the group.

- Are you **the funny one** who makes everyone laugh?
- Are you **the advice-giver** who somehow knows the answers to life's trickiest questions?
- Are you **the peacemaker** who keeps drama under control?

- Are you **the cheerleader** who excites their friends like it's their full-time job?
- Are you **the go-getter** who convinces everyone to actually do stuff instead of just talk about it?

Whatever your special something is, **you matter.** You bring something valuable, even if you haven't quite figured out what it is yet.

And if you don't quite know what it is you bring to the table? No problem! Try new things, learn new skills—and Boom!—you've got a new power to add to your crew!

How to Find and Grow Your Support Social Crew

Hmmmm… so how do you find your people? (Spoiler alert: It doesn't usually happen overnight.)

- **Join Clubs or Groups:** Band? Drama? Chess? Soccer? Debate? Whatever you're into, there's a group for that.
- **Volunteer:** Helping others = meeting people. And normally, they are people who care about important things.
- **Be Open and Friendly:** You don't need to be forever friends instantly, but saying "hi" to someone new? It's a game changer.
- **Use Social Media Wisely:** Be interested in (*follow*) groups that lift you up, not ones that make you feel like you need a whole new personality to fit in.

Leveling Up: How to Keep a Strong Social Support Crew

Once you have a great group, how do you keep it strong? By being great friends, too!

- **Listen Up:** Not everything is about you (wild, I know!). Pay attention when your friends need to talk.
- **Share Your Story:** Being real = stronger friendships.
- **Celebrate Wins Together:** Did your friend finally take a bold step and ask someone out? Hype them up!
- **Be There When They Need You:** Friendship isn't only about fun; it's about supporting people through hard times, too.
- **Keep it Positive:** No one wants to be around a walking rain cloud 24/7. Spread some good vibes.

Why a Support Crew Matters

Your support crew is your team in this wild game of life. They cheer you on, catch you when you fall, and help you grow into the best version of you.

And the best part? You do the same for them.

So, are you ready to find your people? Your power? Your unstoppable squad?

Let's go and make the world shine!

ACTION TAKEAWAYS:

- You need people, and people need you. Together, you're stronger.
- What do you bring to the table? Even if you don't know yet, you bring something awesome.
- Got questions? Talk it out with your parents, a teacher, or someone you trust.

18. Finding Your Squad of Superstars!

Have you ever seen someone walk into a situation and instantly know what to say, how to act, and how to make everyone feel included? Or maybe they're a world-famous soccer player, and they know how to kick the ball like it's attached to a jet rocket. It's like they have some kind of secret superpower! Well, guess what? Those people you look up to? Those are role models!

Role models are like real-life coaches who can teach you how to connect with others, or how to do certain athletic skills, or even show us how to avoid embarrassing social disasters (like accidentally waving back at someone who wasn't actually waving at you… (UGH!))

This chapter is all about finding those people who inspire you to be your best self and help you navigate the world. They can teach you how to have better friendships, learn professional skills, and even help you figure out your goals for the future!

Why Role Models are Like the MVPs of Life

Role models are super important because they show us how to handle situations and skills like a pro. They can inspire us to be the best we can be!

Here's What Makes Role Models So Great:

- **They can inspire you** to do the same things.
- **They Show Us What is Possible:** If they can do it, so can you! They give you tips and tricks to achieve your goals!
- **They teach us how to handle drama:** Learning how they deal with tricky situations can help you keep your cool when things get messy.
- **They Show Us Smarter Ways to Do Things:** Instead of learning "the hard way." A good role model can show you how to do it right the first time.
- **Lead By Example:** Seeing someone achieve their goals can motivate you to achieve your own.
- **They Teach Us How to Bounce Back from Obstacles:** Learning about their struggles and how they overcome them can give you strength during your tough times.

How to Find Your Role Models

- **Look Around:** Role models can be anywhere. Maybe it's a friend, a teacher, a coach, or even a family member.
- **Read Up:** Books, interviews, and videos of confident, adventurous people. These role models can teach you a lot about the world outside your bubble.

Finding Your Squad of Superstars!

- ***"Follow" Wisely:*** Get interested in people on social media who actually inspire you to be your best self, not just the ones who post perfect selfies or drama filled rants.
- **Think Close, Think Far:** Your role model doesn't have to be famous. They could be in your school, in your neighborhood, or even sitting next to you at dinner.

Taylor's Story

"My social role model is my cousin, Alex. He's like the human version of Wi-Fi—he connects with everyone, everywhere, instantly.

"One time, we went to a family reunion, and I was dreading it. I didn't know half the people there, and I was 99% sure I'd be stuck in a weird conversation with some great aunt about my future. (Hello! I am only 12—*eye-roll.*)

"But Alex? He walked right in and high-fived like five people, and suddenly had a whole group of cousins laughing at his jokes. I watched him closely. He asked questions, cracked jokes that weren't mean, and somehow got people talking about their weirdest, funniest stories. He didn't just talk, he listened. And by the end of the night, I was having the best time ever.

"Then there was this time at school when two friends were arguing over who got to pick the team for dodgeball. I was bracing for a major meltdown, but Alex walked up and was so cool and said, 'Okay, fine, you both pick teams. But you have to pick each other first. Deal?' And just like that, all the drama was gone. He's like a walking social Jedi.

"I asked him once how he does it, and he said, 'It's easy! When you make people feel good, they want to be around you.'

"Duh. Why didn't I think of that?"

BIG PRO TIP:

Make sure your role model is worth *following*.

Not everyone who looks like a social superstar is actually worth *following*. Some people use their social skills to manipulate others or cause drama.

How to Spot a Fake Social Role Model

- They only build themselves up by putting others down.
- They're "nice" when they want something, but not all the time.
- They encourage you to do things that make you feel uncomfortable (peer pressure).
- They care more about looking cool than actually doing the right thing.
- They say a lot of noise, but don't actually stand for anything or do anything meaningful.

If someone makes you feel like you have to change who you are just to fit in, they're not someone you should be looking up to. **You don't need to shrink yourself just to fit into someone else's group. You're enough just as you are.**

How to Be a Role Model for Others

It's one thing to find a role model, but what if you were the person everyone wanted to learn from? (Spoiler: You totally can be!)

Once you start mastering your social power, guess what? People might be looking up to YOU to be their role model! Here's how to be the kind of person others look up to:

Finding Your Squad of Superstars!

- **Be Kind:** A simple smile or "Hey, how's it going?" can make someone's day a whole lot better.
- **Be Inclusive:** Don't just stick to your squad. Try to make new people feel welcome.
- **Be Confident, but Not Cocky:** People love being around someone who shares their true self without acting like they're better than everyone else.
- **Master the Art of Awkward Situations:** Instead of cringing when things get weird, learn to smooth them out.
- **Have a Special Skill?** Show others how to do it!
- **Admit When You Messed Up:** Nobody's perfect! If you say the wrong thing, admit it, apologize, and move on.
- **Be the Drama-Free Zone:** Nobody likes the person who's always *stirring the pot*. Be the one who calms the pot down instead.
- **Keep It Real:** People respect those who are honest, but kind. Be the friend who tells the truth without making someone cry.
- **Stand Up for Others:** If someone's being left out or treated badly, don't just ignore it. Be safe, but try to be the one who does something about it. (Get an adult involved if things get out of control. Safety is the number one priority.)

Using Your Voice for Good

Sometimes, being a leader means speaking up when something isn't right. That doesn't mean picking fights. It means using your power in a positive way.

- **Practice courage in small ways.** Start by speaking up in low-pressure situations, like sharing your opinion in class or inviting someone new to sit with you and your group.
- **Stick to facts, not drama.** If you need to call out bad behavior, keep it simple: "That's not fair" works better than yelling "You're being a terrible person!"

- **Look out for your squad.** If you see someone struggling, offer support. Even a simple "Hey, are you okay?" can make a huge difference.

Being a role model isn't about being perfect. It's about being kind, confident, and making sure people around you feel included and respected. The more you learn from great role models, the more you'll become one yourself!

Someone out there might be watching *you* right now, and thinking, "I want to be like them someday." **How cool is that?!**

ACTION TAKEAWAYS:

- Find good role models. Look for people who are confident and kind, not just popular.
- Learn from them. Watch how they handle themselves, and pick up their best skills.
- Avoid fake social power. Don't change to fit in.
- At the end of the day, the best role models are people who figured out how to do great things and help others while still being themselves.
- You can be a role model, too! Keep building your social powers, and you'll be the one that others look up to.

19. Your Social Spark: Bring on Your Own Personal Magic

Let's talk about something extremely important: Your Social Power! You know, that special thing that makes you, well... YOU! The way you talk, joke, think, and interact with people—your whole social vibe—that's your spark! That's your magic!

But here's the deal: The world is packed with all kinds of personalities, and learning to navigate different social situations is like learning how to skateboard. At first, you might totally crash and burn, but once you get the hang of it, you'll be riding it like a pro.

What Does Social Power Look Like?

Social power isn't about being the loudest person in the room or having 50,000 *followers* on TikTok (Although, props if you do!) It's about knowing how to connect with people in a way that's real. Some people are naturally outgoing, while others are more low-key. Some are the life of the party, and some are the ones making sure the party doesn't burn out (a very important job).

Think about your friends: Maybe one is always cracking jokes, while another gives the best advice. Maybe one friend is an introvert who loves books, while another is a full-on extrovert who makes friends with a lamppost. Social power is understanding that all of these personalities are cool and necessary. If everyone acted the same, life would be like a group project where *nobody* has a different idea. (Everyone with the same idea? Boring!!)

Why Should You Care About This?

Because social power isn't just about you, it's about how you interact with everyone else. People remember the way you make them feel. If you make others feel seen, included, and valued, you become the kind of person people want to be around. And guess what? The more you appreciate different personalities, the more you'll appreciate your own.

Skylar's Personal Side Story:

"So, confession time: When I was younger, I thought being 'popular' meant being friends with only the cool people (whatever that means). I thought if I just hung around the right group, I'd somehow become a social superhero. Spoiler alert: I was wrong.

"It all clicked when I moved to a new school. I didn't know anyone and suddenly, I wasn't in the 'cool' group (because, duh, I was brand new). Instead, I actually had to talk to different types of people. And wow, my first real friend? A quiet, artsy girl who could draw better than an actual Disney animator. My second friend? A classmate who was obsessed with science and told me fun facts about black holes at lunch. (I mean, did you know black holes can actually '*spaghettify*' things?! Wild!)

"I started realizing that my real social power wasn't about finding the right group to fit into, it was about connecting with all kinds of people. My world got so much bigger when I stopped limiting myself to only one type of friend. And the funny thing? The more I accepted different people, the more confident I felt about myself."

How Can You Use Your Social Power for Good?

So, now you know social power is a special thing to have. But how do you actually use it?

- **Talk to Someone New:** That quiet kid in class? Ask them what music they like. You might find out that they have some awesome taste in loud-and-proud alternative music!
- **Be a Friend You'd Want to Have:** Don't be the person who only talks to others when they need help with homework. Be the person who checks in, who remembers birthdays, who actually listens.
- **Keep Your Compliments Real:** If you like someone's sneakers, tell them! But don't go overboard with compliments just to impress people. That's like using too many emojis in a text, it gets weird fast.
- **Embrace Your Own Personality:** If you love building robots, love it loudly. If you're obsessed with musicals, sing your heart out. The coolest people? They're the ones who own their differences.

How Can You Help Others Feel Good About Themselves?

Having social power isn't just about standing out, it's about helping others shine, too. Here's how you can be a social superhero:

- **Include People:** Nobody likes feeling invisible. If you see someone standing alone at lunch, invite them over. Worst case? They say no. Best case? You probably made their day.
- **Shut Down Negativity:** If someone's being rude or making fun of someone else, don't laugh along. You don't have to start a fight, but you can change the subject or make it clear that negativity isn't cool.
- **Encourage People to Be Themselves:** If your friend wants to try out for the school play but is nervous, hype them up! Make them feel great about it! Be the reason someone goes for their dreams instead of the reason they hold back.
- **Be Kind—Seriously, Just Be Kind:** It's literally free, and it makes the world a better place.

The Bottom Line

Your social power is yours, and no one can take that from you. It's about knowing who you are is already enough, and that other people's differences don't make them weird, they make them interesting.

So, go out there and own your sparkle! Own your magic! Be open to new people, embrace your quirks, and, most importantly, make the world a little brighter simply by being you!

ACTION TAKEAWAYS:

- Social power is about how you interact with others, not just how popular you are.

- Being open to different types of people makes life much more fun.
- Compliments are great, but only when they're real.
- Don't just be yourself, help others feel good about being themselves, too.
- The world needs all kinds of people, so be the one who celebrates it!
- That's what real social power is: Lifting others up while staying true to who you are.

20. Let's Talk About Something Super Cool: YOU!

Okay, real talk: Have you ever looked around and thought "Ugh! I wish I was more like *that* person!" Maybe they're super athletic, or they can sing like a pop star, or they have the kind of hair that never frizzes (I mean seriously, how??!).

But here's the deal: You're already amazing just by being **YOU!** And not just regular amazing—like, one-of-a-kind, never-seen-before, walking-mic-drop **AMAZING!**

So today, we're talking about what makes you unique, why that's a real superpower, and how to own your specialness like the rockstar you are.

What Makes You Unique?

First things first: What even is *uniqueness*? Well, it's basically what makes you YOU and not a copy of someone else.

Think about it:

- **Your Laugh:** Maybe it's loud, maybe it's a snort laugh, either way, it's iconic!
- **Your Brain:** The way you think, solve problems, and tell jokes—your brain is totally a genius!
- **Your Style:** Whether you love hoodies, neon sneakers, or dressing like a 90s sitcom character. Your style is 100% you!
- **Your Interests:** Maybe you're obsessed with space, can't get enough of writing stories, or can name every dinosaur in history—*Super wow!*
- **Your Personality:** Kind, quirky, energetic, chill—whatever it is, it's yours!

Basically, you're a one-of-a-kind masterpiece, and the world needs every single part of what makes you special.

Why is Being Unique So Important?

Imagine if everyone looked the same, talked the same, dressed the same, and liked the same things. Sounds like a sci-fi movie where robots took over, right? Boring. No thanks.

Being unique makes your life a one-of-a-kind mystery tour! It's what gives the world creativity, different perspectives, and cool ideas. Your specialness isn't just nice, it's necessary.

- **Your creativity?** Could inspire someone to follow their dreams.
- **Your kindness?** Could make someone's day better.
- **Random interest?** Could lead you to an epic adventure.

- **Your humor?** Could make someone laugh when they really need it.

The best part? You don't even have to try to be special. You just are.

PERSONAL SIDE STORY:

Growing up, everyone around me was pretty much the same—same clothes, same music, same everything. It wasn't weird or anything, it's just how life was, and frankly, I didn't know that there was something else out there. You don't know what you don't know, you know?

When I moved to the big city, it was like stepping into a whole new world. Sure, I met a lot of different people in my youth, but my real exposure to diversity came when I moved to a different state.

My first week, I met people from places I'd only seen on maps. A new friend was from a country I couldn't even spell (Sri Lanka). And a girl in ballet could speak three languages like it was no big deal. At first, I felt like a total fish out of water. How was I supposed to connect with people who were so different from me?

But as I got to know them, I realized our differences weren't something to freak out about or get in the way—their differences were actually pretty awesome. My new friend from Sri Lanka introduced me to foods I had never even heard of, and my ballet friend taught me some cool phrases in different languages. We started sharing stories about our lives, and it hit me: Our differences made us way more interesting.

One day, I was sitting in my room reminiscing about fun memories. I was thinking about all the fun things I did with these new and creative people in my life. I realized that, even though we came from totally different backgrounds, we had so much in common. We all had crushes on people, wanted to do fun things, and we all wanted to make the world a better place.

Learning to embrace diversity didn't happen overnight. It took time to get used to, but as I opened up to new cultures, ideas, and people, my world got so colorful. I didn't just learn to accept diversity, I really loved it. It showed me that our differences make the world more interesting, and when we come together, we can do amazing things.

Looking back, I'm so grateful I opened my heart to what made others different, because it helped me see and celebrate what makes me different, too.

How to Own Your Uniqueness Like a Boss

Alright, so how do you actually *love* what makes you different? Here's the cheat sheet:

- **Stop Comparing Yourself:** No one can be you better than **YOU**. Trying to be someone else? You're a limited edition, so own it.
- **Find What Makes You Happy:** If your jam is drawing comics, do it. If you live for baking weird desserts, make those funky cupcakes. Do what makes your heart happy, even if it's not "popular."
- **Be Confident in Your Choices:** Confidence isn't about being the loudest person in the room—it's about knowing you're awesome, whether other people see it right away or not.
- **Remind Yourself Often:** Write down things you appreciate about yourself. Post it on your mirror or the side of your computer screen. Let those reminders make you feel good about yourself every single day.
- **Rock Your Style:** Whether you're totally into kooky socks, vintage jackets, or dressing like an action hero, wear it with pride. Trends come and go, but you? You're timeless. So, wear what makes you feel great!

How to Help Others Feel Unique and Special

Do you want to be a real-life superhero? One of the best things you can do is to help other people feel good about their uniqueness too!

- **Cheer People On:** If someone has an amazing talent, tell them! Compliments are free and powerful. "That was hilarious!" or "Your art is so cool!" can make someone's day.
- **Encourage Individuality:** If your friend wants to try a new style or hobby but is nervous, be their cheer squad! "Dude, that is so cool. Go for it!"
- **Stand Up for Uniqueness:** If someone's getting teased for being different, be the person who says, "Hey, that's actually really cool." You'd be surprised how much power that has.
- **Celebrate Your Own Specialness:** When you show confidence in being you, it gives others permission to do the same. Be the trendsetter!

The Bottom Line

There is literally no one else on this planet exactly like you. Your thoughts, your style, your personality, your laugh—**all of it is a masterpiece.** So, stop trying to fit into some boring mold. Own your quirks. Love what makes you stand out.

> Be yourself; everyone else is already taken.
> — Oscar Wilde

The world doesn't need more *copies*—**the world needs more bold and brave ORIGINALS.** And you, my friend, are an original. Go out there and shine like only you can. The world is much better because you're in it.

ACTION TAKEAWAYS:

- You're one-of-a-kind!
- Being different is a strength, not a weakness.
- Stop comparing yourself. The best thing you can be is yourself.
- Cheer people on! Help them feel confident in their uniqueness too.
- The world needs more originals. That includes you!

21. Let's Shower the World with Kindness

Are you ready to level up your social confidence? Because guess what? Being confident isn't just about rocking your own specialness, it's also about giving back to others and making people feel seen, included, and important. And when you do that? You're empowering your soul! (Whoa! Righteous, yo!)

Being Kind is the Ultimate Superpower

Kindness is like having your very own superpower, except instead of flying or shooting lasers from your eyes (which, let's be honest, is kind of awesome!), you get to change lives with the smallest actions.

Every time you share, lend a hand, or dish out a compliment, you're basically sprinkling magic into the world. And here's the best part—it doesn't only help them, it helps YOU too.

Think of kindness as a hug for your heart. The more you give, the warmer and happier you feel. Scientists even say that being kind boosts your happiness, reduces stress, and makes life feel more meaningful. So yeah, kindness isn't just "nice." It's powerful!

HERE'S A HUGE INSIGHT

This is one of the most important things in this book…

People—ALL PEOPLE—just want to feel special. They want to feel loved…

EVERYONE.

Everyone—including you… me… teachers… policemen… the salesperson that charged you for those jeans you just bought… even someone who's been unkind in the past… everyone.

Simple, right? Seems so obvious. Like, really? But, yes, it's true. And, sadly, that one simple thing is so often ignored.

That one simple thing—making someone else feel noticed and loved—will pretty much define your personal and emotional success in this world.

And, this pursuit of feeling this love come in, and sending out the feeling of love to others, will be a lifelong process.

AND IT WILL BE POWERFUL!

And do you know why it will be powerful? Because it is sincere and because it comes from your heart connecting with someone else's heart. And that's magic in its most powerful form!

What is Currency?

Okay, so here's the deal: Everyone has their own thing that makes them light up like a Christmas tree plugged into an extra long extension cord. It's called their *"currency."* And no, I don't mean money (but yeah, I'll take my allowance early, thank you!)

Currency Is the Emotional Food People Need to Live.

For some people, it's as simple as sharing a snack. Like, you offer them a brownie, and suddenly, you're their new best friend, you're the peanut butter to their jelly. Other people? Compliments. Tell them their hair is giving out "all-star vibes," and they'll be smiling for a week. Others? Maybe it's respect… or attention, or…

The trick is finding out their *thing*. Like, if your friend is obsessed with their pet hamster (seriously, why does it have its own Instagram account?!). If that's important to them, ask them about it. Watch how fast they go from "meh" to "Let me tell you EVERYTHING about Mr. Peanut, the Third."

But hey, here's the best (and sometimes the hardest) part: Finding someone's currency is like going on a treasure hunt, but instead of gold coins, you get happy people. Sometimes, **finding that thing that "turns them on" and "lights them up" is not easy to do**. But, when you find that *thing*, they will perk up like they were plugged into an electrical socket because they will think:

This person actually *SEES* me. They actually *GET* me.

After that, they will really listen to you. They will want to be heard, too. That's how connection happens in a very powerful, positive way. So, get out there and crack their code!

The Great Feeling of Helping Out

Got some time? Share it.

Kindness isn't just about compliments (although it's awfully nice when you get one), it's also about showing up for people.

- **Volunteer your time.** Helping out at a shelter, picking up trash at the park, or reading to younger kids? Instant kindness power-ups.
- **Use your skills for good.** Love math? Help a friend study. A great artist? Draw something for someone.
- **Be the person who includes others.** If you see someone sitting alone or feeling awkward, invite them in. Trust me, they'll never forget it.

You might think these small things don't matter, but trust me, they do.

Make a Difference with Your Small Acts of Kindness

Let's talk about **THE RIPPLE EFFECT.**

Every time you do something kind, no matter how small, you create a ripple—like tossing a pebble into a pond.

Example: You smile at someone… *then* they feel good… *then* they help a friend… *then* that friend is inspired to do something nice for someone else… *then*—BOOM!—kindness is spreading!

Your kindness could inspire a chain reaction of awesomeness. And the best part? You might never know the full impact of the goodness that you started.

PERSONAL SIDE STORY:

I was at the grocery store pushing my cart down the aisles and picking up my favorite snacks. As I reached the checkout line, I noticed a lady in front of me with a worried look on her face. She was counting her money and putting back some of her items because she didn't have enough money to pay for everything.

Feeling a tug at my heart, I leaned forward and said, "Excuse me, but I'd like to take care of your groceries today." The lady looked at me with wide eyes. Her chin quivered, and tears started to form. "Are you sure?" she asked, her voice shaking. "Absolutely," I replied with a smile.

As she left the store, she waved goodbye and had a big smile on her face. I felt a warm glow in my heart. It felt amazing to give back and to help someone else in need. Make a difference with your small act of kindness. It can change someone else's day in a beautiful way.

The Bottom Line

Kindness isn't just some nice thing to do, it's a superpower that makes you more confident, helps you connect with others. It literally changes the world! (WOW! Am I right?)

Ready to Be a Kindness Hero? It All Starts by Saying YES!

ACTION TAKEAWAYS:

- Kindness is your superpower! Use it!
- Making people feel noticed and loved is the secret to life.
- Find people's "currency" and crack their code.
- Small acts create BIG ripples of goodness in the world.
- When people see you being kind, it inspires them to do the same.

22. Most Important Chapter in this Book, and I'm Not Kidding!

Superhero Action—All Month Long, All Year Long, All Life Long!

Hey you, Superstar! Can you believe that we're already at the end of the book? Congratulate yourself on your own personal growth!

I know we've been focusing a ton on what happens as you grow up, and some of it takes getting used to, but here's the scoop—it's important that you keep your vibe high regardless of what you're going through, and let yourself feel awesome, for like, forever!

Let's break down why taking care of yourself and working on your social confidence is so important. Believing in yourself is your secret sauce to rocking your SOCIAL POWER all month long, all year long, all life long.

Who Do You Want To Be When You Grow Older?

Treat yourself and reach for those wild dreams! Go on, you can do it! I'd love to hear all about your success stories!

I ask this now, not because you need to know exactly *WHAT* you want to be when you grow older, but it is important to start figuring out *WHO* you want to be and create that positive mental attitude.

You may not know it, but your adult life has now begun!

Congratulations and Welcome to the Big Show!

Belief in yourself and your skills is a huge part of getting where you want to be in life. What a great time to learn this! While you're adapting yourself to understanding your mind and your body, you might as well apply these same ideas and turn them into some great life skills.

This May Be the Most Important Part of this Book (And I'm Not Kidding!)

Hidden within these chapters are the things I've been writing (and joking around about), dealing with social situations, mastering your social confidence, and taking care of and loving your mind. These are literally the same skills you need to master the skill of life!! (Whaaat?!) Yeah, that's right!

You have all the basic tools in your toolbox now, so rework some of these sentences, wiggle the word "social" out of "My Social Power!" and guess what you're left with—**"MY POWER!"**

That's right! Say it out loud! "MY POWER!!" Scream it, if you want! "MY POWER!!"

Most Important Chapter in this Book, and I'm Not Kidding!

Hahahaha!! I love it! Because, you know what? You can own this, this power of yours. And trust me, I'm not joking with you. When you believe it and you live it—YOU LITERALLY ARE POWERFUL!

So say, "Take that, you crummy puberty dog! You bully monster! You're not going to get the best of me! I've got MY POWER! I've got all these great tools to slay you and any other fire-breathing dragon that comes along!"

Because Building My Social Confidence...

- ... is making me stronger!
- ... is making me wiser!
- ... is making me take care of myself!
- ... is making me understand that all the strength that lies within me is just starting to wake up!

Powerful, isn't it?!

Who knew that growing up was going to be so outrageously important?

Every person that has walked before you has gone through puberty and dealt with social issues, <u>but not every person has understood their power.</u>

I think I should say that again because it is so important!—**not every person has understood their power.**

Please take this beautiful change in your life, and instead of just getting through it, instead of letting it rule you—take your amazing power and own it! Go forth and conquer, my friends!

IMPORTANT: Yes, all of these ideas are great, but you have to apply them to your life to make them work.

I repeat, **YOU HAVE TO APPLY THESE IDEAS TO YOUR LIFE TO MAKE THEM WORK!**

Now Let's Switch Our Talk to YOU Owning All of This Incredible Knowledge!

I NOW KNOW HOW TO:

1. Love my own unique mind and body!
2. Appreciate my friends!
3. Journal my thoughts!
4. Keep my attitude positive!
5. Use life lessons to grow mentally!
6. Appreciate my worth!
7. Not let my emotions rule me!
8. Educate others!
9. Bring something to the table!
10. Be a support to others!
11. Have ideas to handle mean girls, mean guys, and bullies.
12. Create my own support team!
13. Practice positive self-talk!!
14. Say NO to things that aren't right for me!
15. Know the power of setting goals and how to structure them!
16. Think and talk about myself in a positive way!
17. Know I'm not alone!
18. Believe that tomorrow is another day!
19. Practice smart and safe social media rules!
20. Have good people that I look up to!
21. Surround myself with a wonderful support crew!
22. Understand that everyone just wants to feel special and feel loved.
23. Not compare myself to pics I see in magazines or online!
24. NEVER give out my location or sensitive information to people online!
25. Make good choices. Everything in life is choices!
26. Know that kindness is my superpower!

Most Important Chapter in this Book, and I'm Not Kidding!

27. Find great and honorable role models that are worthy of my attention!
28. Celebrate our differences!
29. Know how to handle stress.
30. Combat my inner critic.
31. Be a leader, not a follower!
32. Cut myself some slack!
33. Seek out reliable advice!
34. Talk with my parents or a trusted adult to find the answers to my questions, or to vent my feelings!
35. Learn how to "sell myself," so that my awesome talents, skills and personality will shine!
36. And… **FEEL MY POWER!**

My puberty is only the first step in this beautiful dream we call life. And I understand that what was once "My Social Power!" is now actually me claiming my strength, my body, "<u>MY POWER!</u>"

🖤 🖤 🖤

Thank you for letting <u>*MY SOCIAL POWER!*</u> be a part of this journey with you! I hope you found this book helpful.

Help someone else find the help they need! And you can be the reason for their success!

★★★★★ RATE

1. **Click the Link or Scan the QR Code!**

https://dub.sh/AQQA

2. **Share your feelings:** How did it help you? Did it make you smile? Did you have an "Oh, I get it now!" moment?

3. **Please leave a GREAT STARS ★★★★★ WRITTEN REVIEW** letting everyone know what you loved about the book, so other people will get the help they need also!

4. **Maybe add a picture or video** of yourself to your review and online talking about how the book helped you! I'd love to see who you are! #MySocialPower!

Please also buy:

- **_MY BODY POWER!_** (For Girl Tweens, Teens, and Young Adults)
- **_MY PERIOD POWER!_** (For Girl Tweens, Teens, and Young Adults)
- **_MY SOCIAL POWER! WORKBOOK_** (For Boy & Girl Tweens, Teens, and Young Adults)
- **_MY PERIOD POWER! WORKBOOK_** (For Girl Tweens, Teens, and Young Adults)

These books are the perfect companions for your puberty journey.

Now go out and grab your POWER!

Acknowledgements

Writing **MY SOCIAL POWER!** has been such a rewarding and unforgettable experience, and I owe it to so many incredible people who supported and encouraged me along the way.

First off, an enormous thank you to YOU—yes, *you*, the reader! Whether you're taking your very first steps toward social confidence or you've been on this journey for a while, I'm so proud of you for picking up this book. I wrote every word with you in mind, hoping they would help you feel strong, confident, and empowered in your beautiful skin. You're already amazing just as you are, and I'm so honored to be a part of your story.

To my wonderful family, thank you for being my biggest cheerleaders and reminding me to dream boldly and to go for it. Your love and unwavering belief in me gives me the courage to take on projects like this one. A special shout-out to my parents, who taught me to chase my wildest ideas, embrace confidence, and always practice self-love. Those lessons shaped me not only for this book, but in everything I've written and in everything that I am.

I want to give a heartfelt thank you to Dr. Renee Cotter for writing the thoughtful and powerful foreword and for endorsing **MY SOCIAL POWER!** Your knowledge, compassion, and dedication to your practice have always been inspiring to me. You have empowered many young people and women over many years in your thoughtful and confident way; always calm in response to the questions and needs of others with a kind and listening ear. You're an inspiration to me and to those who know you and have worked with you.

To all the educators, healthcare heroes, and body positivity advocates out there: Your work matters so much. You're changing lives every single day, and your dedication to empowering young people to love and care for their bodies inspires me endlessly. This book is now a part of that beautiful movement you've helped to create.

I also want to shout out to my phenomenal publishing team. You brought this book to life in ways I could only dream of. Every detail is sprinkled with your talent and hard work. I'm so grateful for the care and dedication you poured into making this book come to life.

And to every young reader holding this book, thank you for being curious, brave, and open to learning about yourself. I hope these pages help you navigate the changes, challenges, and joys of growing up with confidence and self-love.

A Special Note to You, the Reader…

You're strong, powerful, and amazing, just as you are. I'm cheering for you every step of the way!

With love and gratitude,

SheriBelle Karper

About the Author

SheriBelle Karper is a true citizen of the world, uniquely equipped to share wisdom on confidence and self-empowerment. For years, she's been an adventure photographer, traveling across the globe (often solo), seeking out new faces, wild places, and unforgettable experiences. She has set foot in a jaw-dropping number of countries! That kind of globetrotting takes some serious confidence.

Through all her travels, SheriBelle has had a front-row seat to some of life's most extraordinary moments. She's danced with tribes in Africa, petted wild Icelandic ponies, and whacked her way through the dense jungles of northern Thailand while trekking alongside elephants. She stood among the solemn bomb sites of Sarajevo, witnessing history's lingering scars, and watched families in Nepal say sacred goodbyes during beautiful afterlife ceremonies. From joy to loss, from wilderness to wonder—she's seen it all.

One of her most unforgettable moments? When she traveled solo to the country of Tonga to freedive in the vast Tongan Trench! (It is the second-deepest ocean trench on Earth, plunging more than an astonishing 35,000 feet. Although, she didn't freedive that far down!) Swimming in those wild, rolling waters—only a few yards from massive humpback whale mothers and their newborn calves—she captured the magic through her professional underwater camera lens. SheriBelle recalls locking eyes with one mother whale, describing it like this: "It felt like I was right there with something god-like, something beyond words, something immensely powerful—like whatever created the sun and the moon... That kind of power? That kind of connection? That kind of adventure? Yep, that takes confidence!

In 2018, when Hawaii's Big Island was first rocked by a volcanic eruption, SheriBelle Karper was right there, capturing history in real time. She spent five intense days behind the lines with the National Guard, shooting alongside media giants like CNN, Fox News, and NBC. Only a few crews were allowed to go back each day, and SheriBelle was among them. Wearing a hardhat, goggles, and a gas mask, she listened as the National Guard's monitors beeped louder and faster—warning of deadly gases in the air. At one point, the wind shifted. She and the team had to sprint to safety, their vans screeching away, just in time. She even took three daring open-door helicopter flights to photograph the lava spewing beneath her. Sitting up front with the pilot, leaning halfway out of the chopper with her camera in hand, SheriBelle captured the breathtaking chaos of that erupting volcano. Fearless confidence, indeed!

But SheriBelle's boldness isn't confined to her global adventures. She's also a multi-award-winning and nominated screenwriter and author, celebrated for her comedic wit and sharp storytelling. She's even taken the mic at Los Angeles's legendary comedy club, *The Hollywood Improv*, performing stand-up for live audiences. Stand-up comedy? That's another arena where confidence is a must!

Her social impact extends beyond the wild and the far away. At home, SheriBelle has spent years empowering young people. She served on the board of a major charity supporting at-risk youth, spearheaded a graffiti-removal program in partnership with a major paint company, and even trained in grief counseling for high school students because she believes so deeply in helping teens navigate life's tough moments.

She's been acknowledged by Los Angeles City and County leaders for her dedication to creating opportunities for teens. She's even enjoyed many years of volunteering at her kids' schools, where she's seen firsthand how confidence and curiosity go hand-in-hand.

And while all of SheriBelle's adventures are extraordinary, her greatest and most fulfilling experience has been raising her two children—her ultimate source of pride. In her words, "They are beautiful and gifted in each their own way, and live fearlessly, with humor and honor." While raising them, SheriBelle has practiced everything she shares in her books, proof that confidence begins at home.

SheriBelle has had all these extraordinary life experiences: From photographing the world's wildest corners to free-diving with whales, to cracking jokes on world-famous stages, to winning awards for her writing, to raising two amazing kids, to fleeing a violent volcano, just to name a few. And somehow, still made it back in time for school pickup. All of these experiences have shaped SheriBelle Karper into a woman who knows what it takes to face life's challenges head-on. She knows that she can trust herself and move through the world with strength and courage. Now, she's bringing that same bold spirit to her writing, crafting confidence guides like ***MY SOCIAL POWER!, MY BODY POWER!, MY PERIOD POWER!, MY SOCIAL POWER! WORKBOOK,*** and ***MY PERIOD POWER! WORKBOOK,*** to help young people discover their own inner power and confidence during this very important time of their lives.

Whether she's swimming with humpbacks, writing award-winning stories, or helping teens embrace their unique journeys, SheriBelle

Karper is on a mission to inspire confidence in all its forms, and she's here to help *you* find yours!

Now it's your turn! What will your adventure be? What kind of confidence are you ready to grow? Whether it's making a new friend, trying something new, or speaking up for what matters to you. This is your moment. Let's go!

Other Titles by SheriBelle Karper...

——YOUNG ADULT——

The MY POWER! Series
https://Dub.sh/MyPowerSeries

MY BODY POWER! (Body Confidence Guide: For Girls - Tweens, Teens and Young Adults) ★★★★★

Also Available In Spanish; Soon in French, German, Italian, European Portuguese, Brazilian Portuguese, Japanese, Simplified Chinese, and Russian

https://Dub.sh/MyBodyPowerBook

MY PERIOD POWER! (Period Confidence Guide: For Girls - Tweens, Teens and Young Adults) ★★★★★

Also Available In Spanish; Soon in French, German, Italian, European Portuguese, Brazilian Portuguese, Japanese, Simplified Chinese, and Russian

https://Dub.sh/MyPeriodPowerBook

MY PERIOD POWER! WORKBOOK (Period Confidence Workbook: For Girls - Tweens, Teens and Young Adults) ★★★★★

Also Available In Spanish; Soon in French, German, Italian, European Portuguese, Brazilian Portuguese, Japanese, Simplified Chinese, and Russian

---

MY SOCIAL POWER! WORKBOOK (Social Confidence Workbook: For Boys & Girls - Tweens, Teens and Young Adults) ★★★★★

Also Available In Spanish; Soon in French, German, Italian, European Portuguese, Brazilian Portuguese, Japanese, Simplified Chinese, and Russian

♥

— —MEMOIR— —

WHY THE WIDOW WEARS BLACK ★★★★★

♥

Please check out all the other titles at

KingmanPublications.com

Kingman Publications LLC

Glossary and Words to Know

Active Listening: Paying full attention to someone, asking questions, and showing you care about what they say.

Ally: Someone who stands up for or supports others, especially when they're treated unfairly.

Assertiveness: Confidently standing up for yourself while still feeling respectful.

Body Language: Nonverbal ways you communicate, like facial expressions, gestures, and posture.

Boundaries: Personal limits you set to protect your time, energy, and feelings.

Bullying: Repeated mean behavior meant to hurt someone physically, emotionally, or socially.

Cliques: Exclusive friend groups that sometimes leave others out on purpose.

Conflict: A disagreement or clash between people with different views or needs.

Conflict Resolution: Finding solutions to arguments or disagreements in a calm, fair way.

Consent: A big deal word that means saying yes or no to things that affect your body. It's about making sure everyone's cool with what's happening.

Cyberbullying: Uses technology and online social media to embarrass, harass, or harm someone.

Diversity: Celebrating and valuing differences in people, like backgrounds, looks, or beliefs.

Empathy: Recognizing and caring about how someone else feels.

Exclusion: Leaving someone out on purpose to hurt or isolate them.

FOMO: (<u>F</u>ear <u>O</u>f <u>M</u>issing <u>O</u>ut) Feeling anxious or upset when you think others are having fun without you.

Gaslighting: Tricking someone into doubting their feelings, memories, or experiences.

Gynecologist: The doctor that you go to for female and related health and problems. They are your go-to source for all period matters. Plus, you will continue to see your gynecologist throughout your adult feminine life.

Inclusivity: Making sure everyone feels welcome and accepted, no matter their differences.

Insomnia: When sleep feels out of reach, and no matter how tired you are, you have a hard time falling asleep or staying asleep.

Kindness: Being thoughtful, caring, and helpful to others.

Meditation: Chilling out on purpose. Sitting quietly and letting your mind take a break from all the noise and busyness.

Mood Swings: When your feelings change super fast, like being happy one minute and sad the next. It can happen around your period because of hormone changes.

Mutual Respect: When two people value each other's feelings, boundaries, and opinions equally.

Overthinking: Constantly worrying about what you said, did, or how others see you.

Peer Pressure: When friends or classmates try to nudge you into doing something you're not so sure about. It's like the pushy friend that tries to convince you to do something that you may not want to do. It is very important to talk to your parents, or a trusted adult, if someone is pressuring you to do something you don't feel is right for you.

Period: Another word for menstruation. It's the few days each month when blood comes out of your vagina, a sign that your body is working right.

Perspective: How someone sees or understands a situation based on their own experiences.

Positive Affirmation: Encouraging words or thoughts that you tell yourself to boost your confidence.

Puberty: The big change-o-rama, when your body goes from kid to teen, getting ready for all the grown-up stuff, like growing hair in new places, getting taller, and starting your periods.

Resilience: The strength to recover and keep going after challenges, setbacks, or tough times.

Respect: Treating others (and yourself) with care, fairness, and dignity.

Rumors: Stories or gossip that spread (without proof) that can be harmful to someone's reputation.

Self-Advocacy: Speaking up for your needs, rights, or opinions in a respectful way.

Self-Awareness: Understanding your thoughts, feelings, and actions, and how they affect others.

Self-Esteem: How you see and value yourself, inside and out.

Social Anxiety: Feeling nervous, worried, or scared about social interactions or being judged.

Social Confidence: Believing in yourself to handle social situations, make friends, and speak up.

Social Cues: Nonverbal hints, like tone or body language, that show how someone feels.

Social Media Safety: Protecting yourself online by being smart about what you post and what you share.

Support System: People that you trust who help you through tough times and cheer you on.

Triggers: Words or actions that can bring up strong, emotional reactions, often tied to past experiences.

Validation: Acknowledging and respecting someone's feelings or experiences as real and important.

Resources & References

Here are some great articles that I enjoyed reading and got a lot of information from. They could be great Resources for YOU!

Take your time and read through them to see which ones might answer your questions.

♥

10 Strategies for Boosting Self-Esteem in Teen Girls: for teachers. (n.d.). https://www.fearlesslygirl.com/blog/10-strategies-for-boosting-self-esteem-in-teen-girls-a-guide-for-teachers

Assistant Secretary for Public Affairs (ASPA). (2025, February 5). *Get help now*. StopBullying.gov. https://www.stopbullying.gov/resources/get-help-now

Atif, H., Peck, L., Connolly, M., Endres, K., Musser, L., Shalaby, M., Lehman, M., & Olympia, R. P. (2022). The impact of role models, mentors, and heroes on academic and social outcomes in adolescents. *Cureus*. https://doi.org/10.7759/cureus.27349

Ayon. (2023, April 28). *The 5 surprising benefits of helping others teens need to know*. HRF. https://www.harrisonriedelfoundation.com/the-5-surprising-benefits-of-helping-others-teens-need-to-know/

Barendse, M. E. A., Cheng, T. W., & Pfeifer, J. H. (2020). Your brain on puberty. *Frontiers for Young Minds, 8*. https://doi.org/10.3389/frym.2020.00053

BBC - Science & Nature - Human Body and Mind - Teenagers. (n.d.). https://www.bbc.co.uk/science/humanbody/body/articles/lifecycle/teenagers/growth.shtml

Blessing, & Blessing. (2020, July 24). *How would you describe or sell yourself? | Lluvia Health*. Lluvia Health - Child and Adolescent Health NGO Nigeria |. https://www.lluviahealth.org/how-would-you-describe-or-sell-yourself/

Boys & Girls Clubs of America. (2024, June 5). *The Importance of Goal-Setting for Teens - Boys & Girls Clubs of America*. https://www.bgca.org/news-stories/2022/January/the-importance-of-goal-setting-for-teens/

Bruce, D. F., PhD. (2023, February 10). *Teens and acne*. WebMD. https://www.webmd.com/skin-problems-and-treatments/acne/what-is-acne

Bryant, C. W. (2023, March 8). *Top 10 things you should not share on social networks*. HowStuffWorks. https://computer.howstuffworks.com/internet/social-networking/information/10-things-you-should-not-share-on-social-networks.htm

CHOC. (2023, June 23). *Social Media Tips for Kids and Teens - CHOC - Children's health hub*. CHOC - Children's Health Hub. https://health.choc.org/handout/social-media-tips-for-kids-and-teens/

Resources & References

Department of Health & Human Services. (n.d.). *Puberty*. Better Health Channel. https://www.betterhealth.vic.gov.au/health/healthyliving/puberty

Dove. (n.d.). *The Dove Self-Esteem Project | DOVe*. htttps://www.dove.com/us/en/dove-self-esteem-project.html?gad_source=1&gbraid=0AAAAADiRVcKsFetkxyFRBX1V7fn0OzrDF&gclid=EAIaIQobChMIodnrpqabiQMVUxitBh0LByFUEAAYASAAEgKu5_D_BwE&gclsrc=aw.ds

Fleming, W. (2024, February 7). *How to help your daughter deal with a mean girl friendship*. parentingteensandtweens.com. https://parentingteensandtweens.com/help-teen-daughter-manage-mean-girl-friendship/

Fremont, E. (2024, October 15). *Which role models will benefit your teens most?* Center for Parent and Teen Communication. https://parentandteen.com/character-role-models/

Garey, J. (2024, August 16). *10 tips for Parenting Preteens*. Child Mind Institute. https://childmind.org/article/10-tips-for-parenting-your-pre-teen/

Girl to Woman: Your Changing Body during Puberty. (n.d.). WebMD. https://www.webmd.com/teens/ss/slideshow-girls-changing-body

Gongala, S. (2024, September 18). *Mean girls at School: types, characters and how to deal with them*. MomJunction. https://www.momjunction.com/articles/how-to-deal-with-mean-girls-at-school_00398481/

Growth and normal puberty. (1998, August 1). PubMed. https://pubmed.ncbi.nlm.nih.gov/9685454/

Healthdirect Australia. (n.d.). *Puberty for girls*. Physical and Emotional Changes | Healthdirect. https://www.healthdirect.gov.au/puberty-for-girls

Helping kids deal with bullies (for parents). (n.d.). https://kidshealth.org/en/parents/bullies.html

How oversharing on social media could put your personal information at risk | Information Technology Services. (n.d.). https://its.uky.edu/news/how-oversharing-on-social-media-could-put-your-personal-information-risk

How to Make Friends - Zen Habits Website. https://zenhabits.net/friends/.

Insightful_Ink. (2023, August 19). Embracing Body positivity: Celebrating diversity for a healthier society. *Mindless Mag*. https://www.mindlessmag.com/post/embracing-body-positivity-celebrating-diversity-for-a-healthier-society

Jd. (2020, December 21). *How Brian Tracy sets goals*. Getting Results. https://gettingresults.com/how-brian-tracy-sets-goals/

Kenny, S. (2020, December 16). *I'm a life coach for teens—this is my advice for handling 'Mean girls.'* Scary Mommy. https://www.scarymommy.com/life-coach-teens-advice-handling-mean-girls

Lmft, E. M. (2024, March 1). How to stop comparing yourself to others: This might be why you feel like you're never good enough. - therapy in a nutshell. *Therapy in a Nutshell*. https://therapyinanutshell.com/how-to-stop-comparing-yourself-to-others/

Ly, C. (2024, January 31). Writing things down may help you remember information more than typing. *New Scientist*. https://www.newscientist.com/article/2414241-writing-things-down-may-help-you-remember-information-more-than-typing/

Making Good Friends - HelpGuide.Org. 2 Nov. 2018, https://www.helpguide.org/relationships/social-connection/making-good-friends.

Mckenzie, E., & Mckenzie, E. (2024, July 26). Acceptance of body diversity: celebrating every shape and size in the fashion world. *East Hills Casuals*. https://www.easthillscasuals.com/blogs/news/accep

tance-of-body-diversity-celebrating-every-shape-and-size-in-the-fashion-world?srsltid=AfmBOoqvDvTilDzru1RmrhuPYnPZdiAlKB3kOKiTHcl-Qx6ABInRtLvH

Myler, C. (2025, February 26). *A shift of priorities for teen boys in high school*. Maggie Dent. https://www.maggiedent.com/blog/a-shift-of-priorities-for-teen-boys-in-high-school/

MyTutor. (2023, May 18). *The psychology of goal setting for teens | MyTutor*. https://www.mytutor.co.uk/blog/parents/educational-advice/goal-setting-for-teens/

National Library of Medicine. (n.d.). *Puberty*. https://medlineplus.gov/puberty.html

"Lack Social Confidence? All Is Not Lost." University of Michigan News, 16 July 2020, https://news.umich.edu/lack-social-confidence-all-is-not-lost/.

Louwagie, L. (2023, July 9). *Home - New Moon Girls*. New Moon Girls. https://newmoongirls.com/

Mayo Clinic Staff. (2023, September 22). *Stress relief from laughter? It's no joke*. Mayo Clinic. https://www.mayoclinic.org/healthy-lifestyle/stress-management/in-depth/stress-relief/art-20044456

Munro, Dan. Why Is Social Confidence Important? | The Inspirational Lifestyle. 31 Jan. 2024, https://theinspirationallifestyle.com/why-is-social-confidence-important/.

Ortega, S., Ortega, S., & Ortega, S. (2022, August 17). *Gaining self-love for teen girls for overall good mental health*. Step up for Mental Health - to Educate. Fight Causes. Change Minds on Mental Health. https://www.stepupformentalhealth.org/gaining-self-love-for-teen-girls-for-overall-good-mental-health/

Parenting, N. (2023, February 6). *Educating teens to make good choices about themselves and their future*. Nurturing Parenting. https://

www.nurturingparenting.com/blog/educating-teens-to-make-good-choices-about-themselves-and-their-future/

Pepper, C. (2025, February 3). *Why adolescent boys are struggling | ParentData by Emily Oster*. ParentData by Emily Oster. https://parentdata.org/adolescent-boys-struggling/

Physical development in girls: What to expect during puberty. (n.d.). HealthyChildren.org. https://www.healthychildren.org/English/ages-stages/gradeschool/puberty/Pages/Physical-Development-Girls-What-to-Expect.aspx

Public Opinion. (2016, December 30). 4-H: Important decisions for teens. *Chambersburg Public Opinion*. https://www.publicopiniononline.com/story/life/2016/12/30/4-h-important-decisions-teens/95753200/

Randi. (2020, December 11). *Why Comparing Ourselves to Others is Dangerous and How to Stop It*. Randi Latzman. https://survivingmomblog.com/trauma-and-hardships/why-comparing-ourselves-to-others-is-dangerous-and-how-to-stop-it/

Reichert, M., PhD. (2023, May 17). Here's what I've learned about raising boys in my 30 years as a child psychologist. *SELF*. https://www.self.com/story/investing-in-the-well-being-of-boys

Robinson, Kara Mayer. "How to Make New Friends." WebMD, https://www.webmd.com/balance/features/how-to-make-new-friends.

Sleep in adolescents. (n.d.). https://www.nationwidechildrens.org/specialties/sleep-disorder-center/sleep-in-adolescents

Schroeder, J. (2023, July 3). 6 Ways Parents Can Help End "The Boy Crisis." *Zooming Out*. https://joannaschroeder.substack.com/p/6-ways-parents-can-help-end-the-boy

Smith, S. S. (2012). The influence of stress at puberty on mood and learning: Role of the α4βδ GABAA receptor. *Neuroscience, 249*, 192–213. https://doi.org/10.1016/j.neuroscience.2012.09.065

Social Media dos & don'ts | North Myrtle Beach, SC. (n.d.). https://www.nmb.us/299/Social-Media-Dos-Donts#:~:text=Always%20verify%20friend%2Ffollower%20requests,anything%20else%20sent%20to%20you.

Staff, N. A. (2025, April 10). *A Parent's Guide to Raising a Teenage Son.* Newport Academy. https://www.newportacademy.com/resources/restoring-families/how-to-deal-with-your-teenage-son/

Styzek, K. (2023, March 12). *3 ways to handle a mean girl - WikiHow.* wikiHow. https://www.wikihow.com/Handle-a-Mean-Girl

The benefits of movement and exercise for teenage girls | Nuffield Health. (n.d.). https://www.nuffieldhealth.com/article/the-benefits-of-movement-and-exercise-for-teenage-girls#:~:text=Encouraging%20your%20daughter%20to%20develop,related%20problems%20as%20an%20adult.

The GMC Group. (2021, August 26). *Teen breathe - breathe.* Breathe. https://www.breathemagazine.com/teen-breathe/

The Royal Women's Hospital. (n.d.-b). *Exercise, diet & periods.* https://www.thewomens.org.au/health-information/periods/healthy-periods#:~:text=A%20healthy%20diet%2C%20avoiding%20salt,reducing%20moodiness%20and%20painful%20periods.

The Ultimate Goal setting Process: 7 Steps to Creating Better goals. (2020, June 15). Lucidchart. https://www.lucidchart.com/blog/7-steps-to-creating-better-goals

Thoughts On Increasing Self-Confidence In Particular Social Situations | Www.Succeedsocially.Com. https://www.succeedsocially.com/confidence.

Thrive Training and Consulting. (2022, November 28). *How Teens Benefit from Helping Others - Thrive Training Consulting.* Thrive Training Consulting. https://www.thrivetrainingconsulting.com/how-teens-benefit-from-helping-others/

Top 10 internet safety rules. (2019, June 18). /. https://usa.kaspersky.com/resource-center/preemptive-safety/top-10-internet-safety-rules-and-what-not-to-do-online

Tagle, A. (2024, August 27). Want to help support your Gen Z kids? Talking really helps. *NPR*. https://www.npr.org/2024/08/27/g-s1-19635/a-new-poll-reveals-the-worries-of-gen-z-kids-and-how-parents-can-support-them

Travers, M. (2023, June 5). *5 things Every teen should know about navigating social media in 2023*. Forbes. https://www.forbes.com/sites/traversmark/2023/06/05/5-things-every-teen-should-know-about-navigating-social-media-in-2023/

User, S. (n.d.). *Eating well: Important for pubertal girls - Puberty2-Menopause*. https://www.puberty2menopause.com/index.php/women-health-resources/i-am-below-18-years-old/puberty/eating-well-important-for-pubertal-girls

Visions. (2023, March 6). *How parents can help Gen Z teens*. Visions Treatment Centers. https://visionsteen.com/how-parents-can-help-gen-z-teens/

Why body positivity is important. (n.d.). https://www.blueridgetreatment.com/post/why-body-positivity-is-important

Why exercise is wise (for teens). (n.d.). https://kidshealth.org/en/teens/exercise-wise.html

Wong, D. (2023, December 16). *How teens can make good decisions every single time (7 proven steps)*. Daniel Wong. https://www.danielwong.com/2023/12/16/how-to-make-the-right-decision/

Writer, P. (2022, March 21). *Teen Body Image - The Dangers of Comparing Yourself to Others - PakMag*. PakMag. https://pakmag.com.au/teen-body-image-the-dangers-of-comparing-yourself-to-others/

Made in the USA
Columbia, SC
21 June 2025